RHODES

TRAVEL GUIDE

2024 EDITION

Rhodes Unveiled: A Comprehensive Traveler's Guide To The Island Of Knights-"Discover The Rich History, Vibrant Culture, And Hidden Gems Of Rhodes"

ROXANNE AZURE

Table of Contents

Introduction   **7**

   Brief Overview of the Island's Significance   8
   What Sets Rhodes Apart   9

Chapter 1   **11**

   Getting Started   *11*
     Geography and Location   11
     Best Time to Visit   13
     Visa and Entry Requirements   16
     Vaccination and Health Precautions   18
     Safety and Security   21
     Budgeting and Money Matters   25
     Essential Packing Checklists   28
     Itinerary Planning for Different Durations of Stay   35

Chapter 2   **39**

   Historical Tapestry of Rhodes   *39*
     The Ancient Roots: Tracing the Millennia of Rhodes' History 39
     Medieval Grandeur: The Era of the Knights   41
     Ottoman Influence and Beyond   42

Chapter 3   **45**

   Geographical Marvels   *45*
     Coastal Wonders: Exploring Rhodes' Breathtaking Shorelines 45
     Inland Beauty: Exploring Rhodes' Majestic Mountains and Verdant Valleys
       47
     Exploring Rhodes' Diverse Landscapes   49

Chapter 4   **53**

   Cultural Mosaic of Rhodes   *53*
     Local Traditions and Festivals: Celebrating the Soul of Rhodes 53
     Arts and Crafts: A Glimpse into Rhodes' Creative Scene   55
     Museums: Unveiling the Tapestry of History and Culture   57

Art Galleries: A Canvas of Expression   59
Modern Influences on Traditional Culture   61

Chapter 5   **65**

Rhodes Cuisine: A Gastronomic Journey   *65*
Savory Delights: Culinary Traditions   65
Must-Try Dishes and Local Specialties   68
Hidden Gems for Food Enthusiasts: Culinary Discoveries Off the Beaten
Path   70

Chapter 6   **75**

Transportation Options   *75*
Getting There   75
Getting Around   77

Chapter 7   **81**

Accommodations Options   *81*
Hotels and Resorts: Comfort and Luxury   81
Villas and Vacation Rentals: Privacy and Flexibility   83
Boutique and Guesthouse Experiences: Personalized Hospitality   85
Budget-Friendly Stays: Affordable Exploration   87

Chapter 8   **91**

Outdoor Adventures and Recreation   *91*
Beach Escapes: Sun, Sand, and Serenity   91
Hiking Trails and Nature Exploration   93
Water Activities and Excursions: Aquatic Adventures   96
Nightlife and Entertainment Hotspots in Rhodes   98

Chapter 9   **103**

Unveiling Hidden Gems   *103*
Off-the-Beaten-Path Discoveries: Secrets of Rhodes   103
Charming Villages and Local Encounters: Authentic Rhodes   106
Rhodes' Best-Kept Secrets: Hidden Treasures Unveiled   108

Chapter 10   **113**

Practical Information and Resources   113
   Essential Contacts and Emergency Information   113
   Recommended Reading and Resources   116
   Sustainable Travel Tips for Rhodes   120

Chapter 11   **125**

   Conclusion   125
   Reflecting on Your Rhodes Experience   125
   Farewell and Best Wishes for Future Adventures   126

Important Note Before Reading

Welcome to our travel guide on Rhodes—an immersive journey designed to captivate your imagination. In choosing not to include images and maps, we aim to:

- Allow your mind to paint the vibrant scenes, fostering a personalized connection with the island.
- Focus on enduring content, ensuring relevance regardless of evolving visuals or mapped routes.
- Encourage free-spirited exploration, embracing the joy of unexpected discoveries.
- Prioritize sustainability by minimizing paper usage and reducing our ecological footprint.
- Inspire genuine connections with locals and fellow travelers by relying on shared experiences.

In the absence of images and maps, we invite you to embark on a visual journey of your own creation. May your adventure in Rhodes be as unique and vibrant as your imagination.

Happy travels!

Introduction

Welcome to Rhodes, a captivating island that beckons you to explore its enchanting landscapes, delve into its rich history, and immerse yourself in the warmth of its vibrant culture. As you step onto its shores, you enter a realm where ancient history, medieval grandeur, and natural beauty converge to create an unforgettable travel experience.

The Warm Embrace of the Aegean:

Rhodes, cradled in the azure embrace of the Aegean Sea, invites you to leave the ordinary behind and embrace a world of wonders. The gentle sea breeze carries the scents of Mediterranean flora, setting the stage for a journey filled with discovery and relaxation.

Diverse Landscapes and Seascapes:

From golden beaches and turquoise waters to rugged mountains and fertile valleys, Rhodes offers a diverse tapestry of landscapes. Whether you're seeking a sun-soaked beach retreat, a hike through pine-scented forests, or a journey to ancient ruins, the island provides a myriad of possibilities for every traveler.

Medieval Charms and Ancient Mysteries:

Rhodes stands as a living testament to the triumphs and tribulations of civilizations past. The medieval city, a UNESCO World Heritage Site, transports you to an era of knights and castles, while ancient ruins whisper tales of a mythological past. Explore the cobbled streets of Rhodes Town and uncover the mysteries that have shaped the island's identity.

Brief Overview of the Island's Significance

Rhodes, with its strategic location, ancient roots, and multicultural heritage, holds a unique place in the annals of history. This brief overview unveils the island's profound significance, shedding light on the factors that have shaped Rhodes into the cultural and historical gem it is today.

Cradle of Mythology:

According to Greek mythology, Rhodes emerged from the sea as a gift from the god Helios to the nymph Rhode. This mythological origin, coupled with the association with Helios and the Colossus of Rhodes, adds a layer of mystique to the island's narrative.

Medieval Fortress and Chivalric Legacy:

The Knights of Rhodes, establishing their stronghold on the island during the medieval era, transformed Rhodes into a formidable fortress. The chivalric legacy of the Knights, evident in the medieval city's architecture, contributes to the island's significance as the "Island of Knights."

Cultural Synthesis and Multifaceted Heritage:

Rhodes' historical tapestry is woven with threads of diverse civilizations, including Greeks, Romans, Byzantines, Ottomans, and Italians. This cultural synthesis has created a multifaceted heritage, reflected in the island's traditions, languages, and communal harmony.

World Heritage Recognition:

UNESCO's recognition of the medieval city of Rhodes as a World Heritage Site underscores its cultural and historical importance.

The preservation of its architectural treasures ensures that the island's legacy endures for generations to come.

What Sets Rhodes Apart

Rhodes distinguishes itself as a destination that seamlessly blends the old and the new, the tranquil and the vibrant. What sets Rhodes apart is not just its historical significance but a combination of elements that create a truly unique and immersive travel experience.

Cultural Fusion in Every Corner:

Rhodes is not merely a relic of the past; it's a living testament to the coexistence of cultures. From the medieval city's atmospheric streets to the lively villages, the island resonates with a harmonious blend of influences that set it apart as a cultural crossroads.

Bountiful Nature and Outdoor Adventures:

Beyond its historical sites, Rhodes captivates nature enthusiasts with its diverse landscapes. Hike through pine-scented forests, relax on pristine beaches, or engage in water sports at vibrant coastal spots—the island offers a plethora of outdoor adventures for every preference.

Warm Hospitality and Local Connections:

The heart of Rhodes beats in the warmth of its people. Whether you're savoring local delicacies in a family-run taverna or engaging in conversation with villagers, the genuine hospitality of Rhodes creates connections that transform a visit into an intimate and memorable experience.

Timeless Traditions and Modern Joys:

Rhodes cherishes its timeless traditions, evident in festivals, crafts, and culinary practices. At the same time, the island embraces the modern world with vibrant nightlife, contemporary art scenes, and a cosmopolitan atmosphere, striking a balance that caters to a diverse array of tastes.

Welcome to Rhodes, a destination where history breathes, nature beckons, and the spirit of the Mediterranean comes alive. As you embark on your journey, may the island's distinctive charms captivate your senses and leave an indelible mark on your travel memories.

Chapter 1

Getting Started

Geography and Location

Welcome to Rhodes, a stunning island in the southeastern part of the Aegean Sea, known for its rich history, diverse landscapes, and vibrant culture. Understanding the geography and location of Rhodes is essential to appreciate the island's unique character.

Geographical Overview:

Rhodes is the largest of the Dodecanese islands, an archipelago of twelve major islands and numerous smaller ones. It sits approximately 18 kilometers (11 miles) southwest of the Turkish coast and about 400 kilometers (250 miles) southeast of mainland Greece. The island's strategic location has played a significant role in its history, influencing its development and cultural influences.

Physical Characteristics:

- Coastal Wonders: Rhodes boasts a diverse coastline that includes long sandy beaches, rocky shores, and secluded coves. The crystal-clear waters of the Aegean Sea surround the island, offering opportunities for swimming, snorkeling, and other water activities.
- Inland Beauty: Moving inland, Rhodes reveals a landscape of mountains, valleys, and fertile plains. The island's highest peak is Mount Attavyros, standing at approximately 1,215 meters (3,986 feet) above sea level. The mountainous terrain contributes to the island's scenic beauty and provides hiking opportunities for nature enthusiasts.

- Historical Significance: The geographical layout of Rhodes has made it a historically significant crossroads. Its position made it a strategic location for trade routes, resulting in a rich history shaped by various civilizations, including the ancient Greeks, Romans, Byzantines, Knights of St. John, Ottomans, and Italians.

Location within the Dodecanese:

- Archipelago Setting: Rhodes is part of the Dodecanese, a group of islands located in the southeastern part of the Aegean Sea. The Dodecanese islands are spread across a wide area, each with its unique character and charm.
- Proximity to Turkey: The island's proximity to the Turkish coast, with the Strait of Marmara to the north and the Mediterranean to the south, has influenced its historical interactions with neighboring regions.

Accessibility:

- Transportation Hubs: The main transportation hub is Rhodes City, situated on the northern tip of the island. The island is accessible by air and sea, with Diagoras International Airport serving as the primary air gateway.
- Ferry Connections: Ferries connect Rhodes to other Dodecanese islands, mainland Greece, and neighboring countries. The harbor in Rhodes City is a bustling hub for both local and international maritime activities.

Understanding the geography and location of Rhodes sets the stage for a deeper exploration of the island's diverse landscapes, historical sites, and cultural heritage. As you embark on your journey through the chapters of this guide, envision the beauty of

Rhodes unfolding before you, inviting you to discover its wonders and immerse yourself in its captivating environment.

Best Time to Visit

Understanding the Seasons

Choosing the best time to visit Rhodes involves considering the island's seasonal variations, each offering a unique experience. Let's delve into the different seasons to help you decide when to plan your trip:

Spring (April to June):

- Weather: Spring is a delightful time to visit Rhodes, characterized by mild temperatures. Daytime temperatures range from 18°C to 25°C (64°F to 77°F), making it comfortable for outdoor activities.
- Floral Beauty: The landscape comes alive with colorful wildflowers, and the countryside is lush and green. This season is ideal for nature lovers and those who appreciate a vibrant, blooming environment.
- Cultural Events: Spring marks the beginning of various cultural events and festivals. It's a great time to witness local traditions and festivities without the peak tourist crowds.
- Outdoor Activities: With pleasant temperatures and fewer tourists, spring is perfect for hiking, exploring charming villages, and enjoying the island's natural beauty.

Summer (July to August):

- Weather: Summer is the high tourist season, offering hot and dry weather. Daytime temperatures can soar to around

30°C to 35°C (86°F to 95°F). The sea temperatures are inviting for swimming and water activities.

- Vibrant Atmosphere: The island is bustling with energy, and beach resorts come alive with visitors. Summer is the peak season for vibrant nightlife, beach parties, and a lively atmosphere.
- Water Activities: Summer is the best time for water enthusiasts, with warm temperatures providing ideal conditions for swimming, snorkeling, and other water sports.
- Cultural Festivals: While the summer months are primarily associated with beach activities, you can still experience cultural festivals and events. However, popular attractions may be crowded.

Autumn (September to October):

- Weather: Autumn brings a gradual decrease in temperatures, with daytime temperatures ranging from 25°C to 20°C (77°F to 68°F). The weather remains pleasant, making it a favorable time to visit.
- Harvest Season: Autumn is harvest season, and you can enjoy fresh local produce. Vineyards are busy with grape harvesting, and local markets showcase an abundance of fruits and vegetables.
- Milder Crowds: As summer draws to a close, tourist numbers decline, providing a more relaxed atmosphere. It's an excellent time for exploring historical sites without the summer crowds.
- Cultural Events: Some cultural events continue into the autumn months, allowing you to experience the island's traditions in a more intimate setting.

Winter (November to March):

- Weather: Winter in Rhodes is mild, with daytime temperatures ranging from 10°C to 15°C (50°F to 59°F). While it's the wetter season, rain showers are typically short-lived.
- Quieter Atmosphere: Winter is the quietest season, making it an appealing choice for those seeking a tranquil getaway. Many tourist services operate at a slower pace during this time.
- Cultural Exploration: Winter allows for a more profound exploration of the island's cultural and historical sites without the crowds. You can enjoy a peaceful visit to museums and archaeological sites.
- Festive Atmosphere: The holiday season brings a festive atmosphere to Rhodes, with Christmas and New Year's celebrations. It's a unique time to experience local traditions and winter festivities.

Factors to Consider:

- Personal Preferences: Consider your preferred weather and the type of activities you enjoy. Whether you prefer the lively atmosphere of summer or the tranquility of winter, Rhodes has something to offer year-round.
- Budget: Prices for accommodation and flights may vary throughout the year. Traveling in the shoulder seasons (spring and autumn) often provides a balance between favorable weather and more budget-friendly options.
- Crowds: If you prefer a more relaxed experience with fewer tourists, consider visiting during the shoulder seasons when the island is less crowded.

- Special Events: Check the local calendar for special events, festivals, or cultural activities that align with your interests.

The best time to visit Rhodes depends on your preferences and the type of experience you seek. Whether you're drawn to the lively beaches of summer, the blooming landscapes of spring, the tranquility of autumn, or the festive atmosphere of winter, Rhodes welcomes you with its diverse offerings throughout the year. Consider the seasons and their unique characteristics to tailor your visit to match your desires and create lasting memories on this enchanting island.

Visa and Entry Requirements

Overview of Visa Requirements

Before embarking on your journey to Rhodes, it's crucial to be aware of the visa and entry requirements for your specific nationality. As of my knowledge cutoff in January 2022, Greece, including Rhodes, is part of the Schengen Area. The Schengen Area is a group of 27 European countries that have abolished passport control at their mutual borders, allowing for easier travel between member states.

Schengen Visa:

- If you are a citizen of a country that is not part of the European Union (EU) or the European Free Trade Association (EFTA), you may need a Schengen Visa to enter Greece and Rhodes. Here are key points to consider:
- Short-Stay Visas: The Schengen Visa is typically a short-stay visa, allowing you to stay in the Schengen Area for up to 90 days within a 180-day period.

- Application Process: You usually need to apply for a Schengen Visa at the Greek consulate or embassy in your home country. Requirements may include a completed application form, passport-sized photos, travel itinerary, proof of accommodation, proof of financial means, travel insurance, and a valid passport.
- Travel Insurance: It's important to have travel insurance that covers medical expenses and repatriation for the entire duration of your stay in the Schengen Area.
- Validity: The validity of the visa depends on your travel plans, but it is usually issued for the specific dates of your intended stay.

Visa-Free Travel:

- EU and EFTA Citizens: Citizens of European Union (EU) member states and European Free Trade Association (EFTA) member states (such as Switzerland, Norway, Iceland, and Liechtenstein) do not need a visa to enter Greece. They are allowed free movement within the Schengen Area.
- Certain Nationals: Citizens of some countries outside the EU/EFTA also enjoy visa-free travel for short stays. However, the specific list of visa-exempt countries can change, and it's essential to check the latest information from official government sources.

Arrival in Rhodes:

- Airport Immigration: When arriving at Diagoras International Airport in Rhodes, you will go through immigration control. Ensure that you have all necessary documents, including your passport, visa (if required), and any supporting documentation.

- Land and Sea Borders: If you are arriving by land or sea, similar immigration controls will apply at the respective border crossing points.

COVID-19 Considerations

- Travel Restrictions: Keep in mind that travel restrictions and entry requirements may be subject to change, especially considering the global situation with the COVID-19 pandemic. Check for any specific COVID-19-related entry requirements, such as testing or quarantine, that may apply at the time of your travel.

Before planning your trip to Rhodes, it is crucial to check the latest visa and entry requirements based on your nationality. Contact the Greek embassy or consulate in your country for the most accurate and up-to-date information. Additionally, stay informed about any travel advisories or changes in entry requirements, especially in the context of the ongoing COVID-19 situation. By ensuring that you have the necessary documents and meeting entry requirements, you can look forward to a smooth and enjoyable visit to this enchanting island.

Vaccination and Health Precautions

General Health Considerations:

Before embarking on your journey to Rhodes, it's important to prioritize your health and well-being. Here are key health considerations and precautions to keep in mind:

Routine Vaccinations:

- Ensure that your routine vaccinations are up to date. These may include vaccinations for measles, mumps, rubella, diphtheria, tetanus, pertussis, and varicella (chickenpox).

Travel Insurance:

- Obtain comprehensive travel insurance that covers medical expenses, emergency evacuation, and repatriation. Confirm that the insurance is valid for the entire duration of your stay in Rhodes.

COVID-19 Considerations:

COVID-19 Vaccination:

- Check the latest travel advisories and entry requirements related to COVID-19. Many countries, including Greece, may have specific entry requirements, including proof of COVID-19 vaccination. Ensure that you are fully vaccinated and carry any required documentation.

Testing Requirements:

- Some destinations may require travelers to undergo COVID-19 testing before departure or upon arrival. Familiarize yourself with the testing requirements of both your departure and arrival locations.

Health Declarations:

- Be prepared to complete health declarations or provide information about your health status, recent travel history, and contact details. This is a common practice to monitor and manage public health.

Health Precautions During Your Stay:

Once in Rhodes, adhere to general health precautions to ensure a safe and enjoyable visit:

Safe Food and Water Practices:

- Consume food and beverages from reputable sources to minimize the risk of foodborne illnesses. Drink bottled or purified water and avoid ice in drinks if you have concerns about water quality.

Mosquito Protection:

- If you are visiting during the warmer months, consider mosquito protection measures to reduce the risk of mosquito-borne illnesses. Use insect repellent, wear long sleeves and pants, and consider staying in accommodations with screened windows.

Sun Protection:

- Rhodes has a Mediterranean climate with sunny and hot summers. Protect yourself from the sun by using sunscreen, wearing hats and sunglasses, and seeking shade during peak sunlight hours.

Medical Facilities:

- Familiarize yourself with the location of medical facilities on the island. Rhodes has hospitals, clinics, and pharmacies where you can seek medical assistance if needed.

Emergency Services:

- Know the emergency contact numbers for medical assistance, police, and other emergency services. In Greece, the emergency number for medical assistance is 166.

Preparing a Travel Health Kit:

Before your trip, assemble a travel health kit that includes essential items such as:

- Prescription medications (with a copy of the prescription)
- Over-the-counter medications (pain relievers, antidiarrheal medications, etc.)
- First aid supplies (bandages, antiseptic wipes, etc.)
- Insect repellent
- Sunscreen
- Personal hygiene items

Consultation with a Travel Health Professional:

- Consider scheduling a consultation with a travel health professional or your healthcare provider before your trip. They can provide personalized advice based on your health history and travel plans.

Ensuring your health and well-being is a crucial aspect of travel preparation. Stay informed about vaccination requirements, especially in the context of the ongoing COVID-19 pandemic. Adhere to general health precautions during your stay, and be prepared with a travel health kit. By taking these measures, you can focus on enjoying your time in Rhodes with peace of mind about your health and safety.

Safety and Security

Ensuring your safety and security is paramount when traveling to any destination, including Rhodes. Here's a comprehensive guide to help you stay safe during your visit:

General Safety Tips:

Secure Your Belongings:

- Keep your valuables, including passports, money, and electronics, secure. Consider using a money belt or neck pouch for essential items.
- Use hotel safes to store valuable items when not in use.
- Be cautious in crowded areas, as these can be hotspots for pickpocketing.

Stay Informed:

- Familiarize yourself with the local emergency numbers and the location of the nearest embassy or consulate.
- Stay updated on local news and any travel advisories for Rhodes.

Emergency Preparedness:

- Have a basic understanding of local emergency procedures.
- Keep a list of important contacts, including the local emergency services, your country's embassy or consulate, and your accommodation.

Cultural Sensitivity:

- Respect local customs and traditions to avoid unintentional offenses.
- Dress modestly when visiting religious sites.

Transportation Safety:

Road Safety:

- Follow local traffic rules and regulations.
- Exercise caution when crossing roads, and use designated crosswalks.

- Be aware of local driving habits and road conditions.

Public Transportation:

- Use reputable transportation providers.
- Be cautious of your belongings on crowded public transport.
- Know the routes and schedules in advance.

Health and Well-being:

Food and Water Safety:

- Consume food from reputable establishments.
- Drink bottled or purified water and be cautious about ice in drinks.

Sun Protection:

- Protect yourself from the sun, especially during hot summer months.
- Use sunscreen, wear hats, and seek shade when necessary.

Medical Services:

- Identify the location of medical facilities and pharmacies.
- Carry a basic first aid kit and any necessary prescription medications.

Local Laws and Customs:

Legal Considerations:

- Familiarize yourself with local laws and regulations.
- Respect local customs, and be aware of any cultural taboos.

Drug Laws:

- Be aware of local drug laws, as penalties can be severe.

Natural Disasters:

Earthquakes:

- While rare, Greece is prone to earthquakes. Familiarize yourself with safety procedures in case of seismic activity.
- Follow local guidance in the event of an earthquake.

COVID-19 Considerations:

Health and Safety Protocols:

- Adhere to any COVID-19-related health and safety protocols, including mask-wearing and social distancing.
- Stay informed about testing and vaccination requirements.

Socializing Safely:

Nightlife Safety:

- Exercise caution when enjoying the nightlife. Be aware of your surroundings and avoid poorly lit or unfamiliar areas.
- Stay in groups, especially in less crowded areas.

Alcohol Consumption:

- Drink responsibly and be aware of your alcohol tolerance.
- Be cautious about accepting drinks from strangers.

Rhodes is generally a safe destination for travelers, but it's essential to prioritize your safety through awareness and preparedness. Stay informed, follow local guidelines, and exercise common sense during your visit. By taking these precautions, you can fully enjoy the beauty and cultural richness of Rhodes while ensuring a secure and memorable experience.

Budgeting and Money Matters

Planning your budget is a crucial aspect of any travel experience. Here's a comprehensive guide to help you manage your finances during your visit to Rhodes:

Currency and Payment Methods:

Currency:

- The official currency in Greece, including Rhodes, is the Euro (EUR). Familiarize yourself with current exchange rates before your trip.

Payment Methods:

- Credit cards are widely accepted in tourist areas, hotels, and larger establishments. Visa and Mastercard are the most commonly accepted. However, it's advisable to carry some cash for smaller establishments and local markets.

Budgeting for Accommodation:

Accommodation Options:

- Rhodes offers a range of accommodation options, from luxury hotels to budget-friendly guesthouses and hostels.
- Research and book accommodations in advance to secure the best rates.

Seasonal Price Variations:

- Prices for accommodations may vary based on the season. Consider traveling during the shoulder seasons (spring and autumn) for potentially lower rates.

Dining and Food Expenses:

Dining Options:

- Rhodes has a diverse culinary scene with options ranging from upscale restaurants to traditional tavernas and local eateries.
- Dining in local establishments can be more budget-friendly than tourist-centric areas.

Self-Catering:

- If your accommodation allows, consider self-catering for some meals. Visit local markets for fresh produce and ingredients.

Drinking Water:

- Tap water in Rhodes is generally safe to drink, but many prefer bottled water. Factor water expenses into your daily budget.

Transportation Costs:

Local Transportation:

- Public buses and taxis are common modes of local transportation. Check fare prices and plan your transportation budget accordingly.

Car Rentals:

- If you plan to rent a car for exploring the island, include rental fees, fuel costs, and any parking expenses in your budget.

Activities and Attractions:

Entrance Fees:

- Research the entrance fees for attractions and historical sites you plan to visit.
- Some sites may offer discounted rates for students or certain age groups.

Guided Tours:

- If you're interested in guided tours, factor these costs into your budget. Prices may vary based on the type and duration of the tour.

Miscellaneous Expenses:

Souvenirs and Shopping:

- Allocate a portion of your budget for souvenirs and local products.
- Bargaining may be common in local markets, so be prepared for negotiation.

Communication Costs:

- Consider communication costs such as SIM cards or international roaming fees for your mobile phone.

Emergency Fund:

- Set aside a small emergency fund for unexpected expenses or contingencies.

Money-Saving Tips:

Local Markets:

- Shop for fresh produce, snacks, and souvenirs at local markets for potentially lower prices than tourist areas.

Free Activities:

- Take advantage of free or low-cost activities, such as exploring public beaches, walking tours, or hiking trails.

Dining Strategically:

- Consider having your main meal at lunchtime when some restaurants offer more affordable lunch menus.

Creating a detailed budget and managing your expenses wisely will enhance your overall travel experience in Rhodes. Research prices, plan ahead, and be mindful of your spending to make the most of your budget while enjoying the beauty and culture that the island has to offer.

Essential Packing Checklists

Efficient packing is key to a smooth and enjoyable trip. Here's a detailed checklist to ensure you have everything you need for your visit to Rhodes:

Travel Documents:

- Passport (with at least six months' validity beyond your planned departure date)
- Visa (if required)
- Travel insurance documents
- Flight tickets
- Hotel reservation confirmations
- Photocopies of important documents (stored separately)

Money and Finances:

- Euros (cash) and credit/debit cards
- Money belt or travel pouch for valuables

- Travel wallet or organizer for documents and receipts
- International adapter for electronic devices
- Budgeting spreadsheet or travel expense tracker

Clothing and Accessories:

- Lightweight and comfortable clothing suitable for the season
- Swimwear
- Comfortable walking shoes or sandals
- Hat and sunglasses
- Light jacket or sweater for cooler evenings
- Travel-sized laundry detergent (for longer stays)
- Umbrella or raincoat (depending on the season)
- Sleepwear

Toiletries and Personal Care:

- Toothbrush and toothpaste
- Shampoo and conditioner
- Body wash or soap
- Deodorant
- Razor and shaving cream
- Sunscreen (with a high SPF)
- Moisturizer
- Personal medications and a small first aid kit
- Feminine hygiene products
- Insect repellent

Electronics and Gadgets:

- Mobile phone and charger
- Camera or smartphone for photos

- Power bank for recharging devices on the go
- Travel-sized power strip with multiple outlets
- Headphones
- E-reader or tablet (optional)
- Adapters for electronic devices

Entertainment and Travel Comfort:

- Book or e-reader
- Travel pillow
- Earplugs and sleep mask
- Travel-sized games or entertainment
- Portable water bottle
- Snacks and refreshments for the journey

Sightseeing and Exploration:

- Daypack or small backpack for daily outings
- Map of Rhodes and guidebook
- Sunglasses and sunscreen for outdoor activities
- Lightweight and foldable reusable shopping bag
- Portable, refillable water bottle
- Snacks for energy on the go

Miscellaneous Items:

- Luggage locks
- Travel-sized sewing kit
- Ziplock bags for organizing items and potential spills
- Travel-sized laundry detergent
- Compact travel umbrella
- Multipurpose tool or Swiss Army knife (pack in checked luggage)

Health and Safety:

- Prescription medications and a copy of prescriptions
- Basic first aid kit
- Personal identification with emergency contact information
- Allergy medication or EpiPen if applicable
- Hand sanitizer or wet wipes

Clothing and Gear for Specific Activities (if applicable):

- Hiking shoes and gear for nature walks or trails
- Snorkel gear for beach outings
- Yoga mat or exercise equipment if planning fitness activities
- Specialized clothing or gear for specific activities (e.g., scuba diving, cycling)

Important Reminders:

- Check the weather forecast for Rhodes before packing.
- Pack travel-sized toiletries to save space and comply with airline regulations.
- Roll clothing to save space and reduce wrinkles.
- Consider the weight restrictions for your airline and pack accordingly.
- Pack a change of clothes and essential items in your carry-on in case of luggage delays.

By following this comprehensive packing checklist, you can ensure that you have everything you need for a comfortable and enjoyable trip to Rhodes. Tailor the checklist to your specific needs and the activities you plan to engage in during your stay. Safe travels!

Essential Useful Phrases

While English is widely spoken in tourist areas, making an effort to learn some basic Greek phrases can greatly enhance your experience and interactions in Rhodes. Here's a list of essential phrases to help you communicate effectively:

Greetings and Polite Expressions:

- Hello/Hi - Γεια σας (Yia sas)
- Good morning - Καλημέρα (Kalimera)
- Good afternoon - Καλησπέρα (Kalispera)
- Good evening - Καληνύχτα (Kalinihta)
- Goodbye - Αντίο (Adio)
- Please - Παρακαλώ (Parakalo)
- Thank you - Ευχαριστώ (Efharisto)
- Excuse me/Sorry - Συγγνώμη (Signomi)
- Yes - Ναι (Ne)
- No - Όχι (Ochi)

Basic Communication:

- Do you speak English? - Μιλάτε αγγλικά; (Milate anglika?)
- I don't understand - Δεν καταλαβαίνω (Den katalaveno)
- What is your name? - Πώς σας λένε; (Pos sas lene?)
- My name is... - Με λένε... (Me lene...)
- How are you? - Πώς είστε; (Pos iste?)
- I'm fine, thank you - Καλά, ευχαριστώ (Kala, efharisto)
- Where is...? - Πού είναι...; (Pou ine...?)
- How much does this cost? - Πόσο κοστίζει αυτό; (Poso kostizei auto?)
- Can you help me? - Μπορείτε να με βοηθήσετε; (Boreite na me voithisete?)

- I need... - Χρειάζομαι... (Hriazome...)

Ordering Food and Drinks:

- Menu, please - Κάνετε μου το μενού, παρακαλώ (Kanete mou to menu, parakalo)
- I would like... - Θα ήθελα... (Tha ithela...)
- Water - Νερό (Nero)
- Wine - Κρασί (Krasi)
- Beer - Μπύρα (Bira)
- Coffee - Καφές (Kafes)
- Tea - Τσάι (Tsai)
- Bill, please - Τον λογαριασμό, παρακαλώ (Ton logariasmo, parakalo)
- Delicious - Νόστιμο (Nostimo)
- Can I have the check? - Μπορώ να πάρω τον λογαριασμό; (Boro na paro ton logariasmo?)

Getting Around:

- Where is the bus station? - Πού είναι η στάση του λεωφορείου; (Pou ine i stasi tou leoforeiou?)
- Taxi - Ταξί (Taxi)
- How much to go to...? - Πόσο για να πάω στο...; (Poso ya na pao sto...?)
- Left - Αριστερά (Aristera)
- Right - Δεξιά (Dexia)
- Straight ahead - Κατευθείαν (Kateuthian)
- Where is the nearest pharmacy? - Πού είναι η πλησιέστερη φαρμακείο; (Pou ine i plisioteri farmakeio?)
- I need a map - Χρειάζομαι ένα χάρτη (Hriazome ena charti)
- Train station - Σταθμός τρένου (Stathmos trenou)

- Airport - Αεροδρόμιο (Aerodromio)

Emergency Phrases:

- Help! - Βοήθεια! (Voithia!)
- I need a doctor - Χρειάζομαι γιατρό (Hriazome yatro)
- Emergency - Έκτακτη ανάγκη (Ektakti anagi)
- I've lost my passport - Έχω χάσει το διαβατήριό μου (Eho hasei to diavaterio mou)
- Police - Αστυνομία (Astynomia)
- I'm not feeling well - Δεν αισθάνομαι καλά (Den aisthanomai kala)
- Fire - Πυρκαγιά (Pirkagia)
- Where is the nearest hospital? - Πού είναι το πλησιέστερο νοσοκομείο; (Pou ine to plisiotero nosokomeio?)
- I've been robbed - Με ληστέψανε (Me listepsane)
- Call the embassy - Καλέστε την πρεσβεία (Kaleste tin presveia)

Cultural Phrases:

- Thank you very much - Σας ευχαριστώ πολύ (Sas efharisto poli)
- You're welcome - Παρακαλώ (Parakalo)
- Cheers! - Στην υγεία σας! (Stin igia sas)
- Enjoy your meal - Καλή όρεξη (Kali orexi)
- Congratulations - Συγχαρητήρια (Sygharitiria)

Learning a few basic Greek phrases shows respect for the local culture and can enhance your travel experience in Rhodes. While many locals speak English, the effort to communicate in their language is often appreciated. Practice these phrases and enjoy engaging with the warm and welcoming people of Rhodes. Safe travels!

Itinerary Planning for Different Durations of Stay

Planning your itinerary is a crucial part of ensuring a fulfilling and enjoyable experience in Rhodes. Here's a detailed guide for different durations of stay, including weekend getaways, a week-long stay, and extended stays:

Weekend Getaway: 2-3 Days

Day 1: Arrival and Old Town Exploration

- Morning: Arrive in Rhodes and check into your accommodation.
- Afternoon: Explore the UNESCO-listed Old Town. Visit the Palace of the Grand Master and stroll through the medieval streets.
- Evening: Enjoy dinner in a traditional taverna.

Day 2: Coastal Beauty and Relaxation

- Morning: Head to Lindos and explore the Acropolis.
- Afternoon: Relax on the beaches of Lindos or Anthony Quinn Bay.
- Evening: Return to Rhodes Town for dinner at a seaside restaurant.

Day 3: Nature and Departure

- Morning: Visit the Valley of the Butterflies.
- Afternoon: Explore the ruins of Kamiros.
- Evening: Relax in a local café before departing.

Week-Long Stay: 7 Days

Day 1-2: Rhodes Town and Old Town

- Spend the first two days exploring Rhodes Town, including the Old Town, the Archaeological Museum, and the Street of the Knights.

Day 3: Lindos and Acropolis

- Take a day trip to Lindos, visit the Acropolis, and explore the charming village.

Day 4: Relaxation on the East Coast

- Spend a day at Tsambika Beach or Anthony Quinn Bay, enjoying the sun and water.

Day 5: Nature and History

- Explore the Valley of the Butterflies and the ruins of Kamiros.

Day 6: Western Coast and Monolithos Castle

- Discover the picturesque villages on the western coast and visit Monolithos Castle.

Day 7: Leisure and Departure

- Spend your last day leisurely, perhaps shopping for souvenirs. Depart in the evening.

Extended Stay: 2 Weeks or More

Week 1: Cultural Immersion

- Explore Rhodes Town, including the Old Town and museums.

- Day trips to Lindos, Kamiros, and the Valley of the Butterflies.
- Attend local festivals or events happening during your stay.

Week 2: Island Exploration

- Visit lesser-known villages like Emponas and Archangelos.
- Explore the natural beauty of Seven Springs and Profitis Ilias.
- Embark on a boat trip to Symi or Chalki for a day.

Weeks 3 and Beyond: Slow Exploration and Local Living

- Venture into lesser-explored areas like Kritinia and Apollona.
- Attend local markets and cooking classes to immerse in the cuisine.
- Join community events or workshops to connect with locals.

Tips for Itinerary Planning:

- Consider Interests: Tailor your itinerary to your interests, whether it's history, nature, or relaxation.
- Balance Activity and Relaxation: Plan a mix of sightseeing and downtime to avoid burnout.
- Local Events: Check for local festivals or events during your stay for a cultural experience.
- Weather Considerations: Be mindful of the weather, especially during the peak summer months.
- Transportation: Plan transportation in advance, especially for day trips or exploring remote areas.

Whether you have a weekend, a week, or an extended stay, Rhodes offers a diverse range of experiences. Customize your itinerary based on your preferences, and don't hesitate to explore beyond the well-trodden paths to discover the hidden gems of this enchanting island.

Chapter 2

Historical Tapestry of Rhodes

The Ancient Roots: Tracing the Millennia of Rhodes' History

Rhodes, with its sun-kissed shores and vibrant culture, has a history that extends far beyond the medieval period. To truly appreciate the island's allure, one must embark on a journey through its ancient roots, where myth and history intertwine to shape the foundation of Rhodes' captivating narrative.

Prehistoric Settlements:

The earliest evidence of human habitation on Rhodes dates back to the Neolithic period, around 4,000 BCE. Archaeological excavations have unearthed remnants of prehistoric settlements, revealing the island's ancient roots as a home to early civilizations.

Minoan Influence:

Rhodes, strategically located at the crossroads of major ancient sea routes, attracted the attention of the Minoans from Crete. The Minoan civilization left its mark on the island, evident in archaeological finds such as pottery and artifacts, showcasing a maritime connection that would become integral to Rhodes' identity.

Dorian Settlement and the Founding of Rhodes City:

Around the 8th century BCE, Dorians, a Greek-speaking people, established a settlement on the northern tip of the island. This marked the beginning of the city of Rhodes. The Dorians, recognizing the island's fertile land and advantageous position, laid the groundwork for the island's future prosperity.

Rhodes in the Classical Period:

As part of the Delian League, Rhodes thrived during the Classical period. The island contributed both ships and resources, and its naval prowess played a crucial role in the league's endeavors. The Colossus of Rhodes, one of the Seven Wonders of the Ancient World, was erected during this time, serving as a testament to the island's grandeur.

Hellenistic Era and the Rise of the Rhodian Navy:

Rhodes reached the height of its power and influence during the Hellenistic era. The Rhodian Navy emerged as a formidable force, protecting trade routes and ensuring the island's economic prosperity. The city of Rhodes became a center for commerce and culture, attracting scholars, artists, and philosophers.

Roman and Byzantine Periods:

With the decline of the Roman Empire, Rhodes experienced a shift in power dynamics. The island transitioned to Byzantine rule, leaving behind structures such as the Byzantine Fort of Monolithos as testaments to this era. The ancient roots of Rhodes continued to evolve, shaped by successive civilizations.

Exploring the ancient roots of Rhodes unveils a tapestry woven with the threads of prehistoric settlements, classical grandeur, and maritime prominence. The remnants of this rich history, scattered across the island, invite travelers to delve into the mysteries and marvels that have shaped Rhodes over millennia.

Medieval Grandeur: The Era of the Knights

Rhodes boasts a storied history that spans millennia, but it was during the medieval period that the island reached the zenith of its grandeur. At the heart of this era lies the captivating tale of the Knights of Rhodes, a chapter that left an indelible mark on the island's landscape and culture.

The Arrival of the Knights:

In the early 14th century, the Knights Hospitaller, also known as the Knights of St. John, arrived on Rhodes. Seeking refuge after being expelled from Jerusalem, the Knights established their headquarters on the island. This strategic location was pivotal for their defense against the Ottoman Empire and other maritime threats.

The Construction of the Grand Master's Palace:

One of the most iconic structures from this period is the Grand Master's Palace in Rhodes Town. Built in the 14th century, the palace served as the residence of the Grand Master and the administrative center of the Knights. Its architecture reflects a blend of Gothic, Renaissance, and Ottoman influences, showcasing the cosmopolitan nature of Rhodes during this time.

The Fortifications of Rhodes:

Recognizing the strategic importance of the island, the Knights undertook extensive fortification projects. The result was a formidable defensive system that included the Palace of the Grand Master, the Street of the Knights, and the imposing walls that surrounded the medieval city of Rhodes. These fortifications withstood numerous sieges, including the famous Siege of Rhodes in 1522.

The Street of the Knights:

Strolling along the cobblestone Street of the Knights is like stepping back in time. Lined with medieval inns that once housed the various langues (tongues or nationalities) of the Knights, the street exudes an aura of chivalry and nobility.

The End of the Knights' Rule:

Despite their valiant efforts, the Knights eventually succumbed to the Ottoman forces in 1522 after a prolonged siege. The surrender marked the end of their rule on Rhodes, and the island became part of the Ottoman Empire.

Legacy of the Knights:

The legacy of the Knights of Rhodes lives on in the island's architecture, culture, and even in its name. The Street of the Knights stands as a testament to their medieval prowess, and the Grand Master's Palace is a symbol of their influence. Today, visitors can explore these historic sites, immersing themselves in the medieval ambiance that still lingers in Rhodes.

Understanding the medieval grandeur of Rhodes provides a key to unlocking the island's cultural richness. The legacy of the Knights, woven into the very fabric of Rhodes, continues to fascinate and inspire those who delve into the island's historical tapestry.

Ottoman Influence and Beyond

As the medieval era drew to a close, Rhodes witnessed a transformative shift in its history with the arrival of the Ottoman Empire. The period following the Knights' surrender in 1522 marked the beginning of a new chapter for the island, characterized by Ottoman influence, cultural assimilation, and a legacy that resonates through the centuries.

The Ottoman Conquest:

Following a prolonged siege, the Knights Hospitaller, exhausted and outnumbered, surrendered Rhodes to the Ottoman forces in 1522. The Ottomans, under the command of Suleiman the Magnificent, took control of the island, bringing an end to the Knights' rule. This marked the beginning of a period of Ottoman dominance that would shape Rhodes for nearly four centuries.

Architectural Adaptations:

Under Ottoman rule, Rhodes underwent architectural transformations influenced by Islamic aesthetics. Mosques, minarets, and Turkish baths emerged alongside existing medieval structures. The iconic Suleymaniye Mosque, built during this period, stands as a symbol of the island's adaptation to Ottoman architectural styles.

Cultural Synthesis:

The Ottoman era on Rhodes witnessed a cultural synthesis as the island became a meeting point for Eastern and Western influences. The diverse population, comprising Greeks, Turks, Jews, and Italians, contributed to a rich tapestry of traditions, languages, and customs. This multicultural environment left an indelible mark on the island's identity.

Economic Flourish and Decline:

Despite the initial economic flourish under Ottoman rule, with Rhodes serving as a significant trade hub, the island experienced a decline in the subsequent centuries. Factors such as piracy, earthquakes, and changing trade routes contributed to Rhodes losing its prominence as a commercial center.

The Italian Period:

In 1912, Rhodes became part of the Italian Dodecanese, following the Italo-Turkish War. During the Italian occupation, significant infrastructural changes occurred, with the Italians leaving their mark on the island's urban planning and architecture. Italian influence is evident in buildings such as the Governor's Palace in Rhodes Town.

World War II and Post-War Period:

Rhodes faced challenges during World War II, enduring bombings and occupation by Axis forces. The end of the war saw the Dodecanese islands coming under British administration before ultimately being integrated into the modern Greek state in 1947.

Legacy of Ottoman Influence:

The Ottoman legacy endures in Rhodes' cultural landscape. From Turkish baths to elements of Ottoman architecture, the island serves as a living testament to the centuries of coexistence and shared history between different civilizations.

The Ottoman influence and the subsequent periods of change have shaped Rhodes into the multifaceted destination it is today. Exploring the island's historical tapestry provides a nuanced understanding of how successive civilizations have left their mark on this captivating Mediterranean jewel.

Chapter 3

Geographical Marvels

Coastal Wonders: Exploring Rhodes' Breathtaking Shorelines

Rhodes, blessed with a diverse and stunning coastline, beckons travelers with its coastal wonders. From pristine beaches and secluded coves to dramatic cliffs and crystal-clear waters, the island's maritime beauty invites exploration and relaxation alike.

The East Coast Beaches:

The eastern shores of Rhodes boast some of the island's most popular beaches. Faliraki, with its golden sands and vibrant atmosphere, is a hub for water sports and beachside entertainment. Further south, Tsambika Beach captivates visitors with its long stretch of soft sand framed by lush hills.

Lindos and St. Paul's Bay:

The picturesque village of Lindos on the southeast coast is not only a historical gem but also home to captivating beaches. St. Paul's Bay, nestled below the Acropolis of Lindos, offers a serene setting with its turquoise waters and views of the ancient ruins.

Prassonisi Peninsula:

For those seeking a more adventurous coastal experience, the Prassonisi Peninsula at the southern tip of Rhodes is a must-visit. Here, the Aegean and Mediterranean Seas converge, creating ideal conditions for windsurfing and kitesurfing. The surrounding beaches provide a unique blend of rugged beauty and water sports excitement.

Anthony Quinn Bay:

Named after the famous actor who fell in love with Rhodes during the filming of "The Guns of Navarone," Anthony Quinn Bay is a hidden gem on the island. This small, rocky cove boasts emerald-green waters, excellent snorkeling opportunities, and a tranquil ambiance.

Afandou Beach and Kolymbia Bay:

Moving to the northern part of Rhodes, Afandou Beach offers a long stretch of pebble and sand, ideal for those seeking a more secluded coastal escape. Nearby, Kolymbia Bay enchants with its calm waters and scenic surroundings, making it a perfect spot for a leisurely day by the sea.

West Coast Charms:

The west coast of Rhodes unveils its own set of coastal wonders. From the vibrant beaches of Ialyssos and Ixia, where water sports enthusiasts can indulge in their favorite activities, to the peaceful shores of Kritinia with its medieval castle backdrop, the west coast offers a diverse range of experiences.

Pristine Secluded Coves:

Beyond the popular beaches, Rhodes is adorned with numerous hidden coves waiting to be discovered. These secluded gems, often accessible by boat or a short hike, offer a more intimate connection with nature. Seek out places like Ladiko Bay or Traganou Beach for a serene escape.

Sunset at Kamiros Skala:

Along the western coast, the ancient harbor of Kamiros Skala provides a spectacular setting to witness the sun sinking into the

Aegean Sea. The combination of ancient ruins and a tranquil coastal atmosphere makes it a captivating spot for both history enthusiasts and sunset seekers.

Rhodes' coastal wonders create a tapestry of experiences, whether you're in search of vibrant beach life, water sports adventures, or peaceful moments in secluded coves. The island's diverse shores invite exploration, promising unforgettable moments along its mesmerizing coastline.

Inland Beauty: Exploring Rhodes' Majestic Mountains and Verdant Valleys

Beyond the enchanting coastline, Rhodes reveals an often-overlooked facet of its beauty – the inland landscapes of majestic mountains and verdant valleys. This chapter invites you to venture off the beaten path and discover the hidden treasures that lie within the heart of the island.

Mount Attavyros: The Summit of Rhodes:

At the heart of Rhodes, Mount Attavyros stands as the island's highest peak, reaching an elevation of approximately 1,215 meters. Ascending its slopes provides not only a physical challenge but a journey through changing ecosystems. From olive groves to pine forests, the ascent unveils the island's diverse flora.

Pine-Clad Slopes and Aromatic Forests:

As you ascend the mountains, the landscape transforms into dense pine forests. The aroma of resin fills the air, creating a sensory experience that complements the visual feast of lush greenery. These forests are not only aesthetically pleasing but also vital for the island's ecosystem.

Filerimos Hill: A Historical and Natural Oasis:

Filerimos Hill, situated between Ialyssos and Kremasti, is a captivating blend of history and natural beauty. The cypress-lined path leading to the ancient acropolis offers panoramic views of the surrounding valleys and the Aegean Sea, creating a serene setting for reflection and exploration.

Butterfly Valley: A Verdant Sanctuary:

Descending from the mountainous interior, Butterfly Valley (Petaloudes) is a natural wonder. During the summer months, thousands of Jersey Tiger moths inhabit the valley, creating a spectacular display of colors. The lush greenery, streams, and waterfalls contribute to the valley's enchanting ambiance.

Kritinia: A Mountain Village with a View:

Nestled on the slopes of Mount Profitis Ilias, the village of Kritinia offers not only traditional charm but also panoramic views of the western coast. Surrounded by verdant landscapes, Kritinia provides a tranquil retreat for those seeking a peaceful escape into the island's inland beauty.

Valleys of Abundant Agriculture:

Rhodes' valleys are not only visually stunning but also serve as fertile grounds for agriculture. Olive groves, vineyards, and orchards blanket the valleys, contributing to the island's agricultural bounty. The cultivation of olives, grapes, and other produce is deeply intertwined with Rhodes' cultural and culinary heritage.

Seven Springs (Epta Piges): A Oasis in the Mountains:

Tucked away in a wooded area, the Seven Springs is a refreshing oasis in the midst of the mountains. Natural springs converge to form a small lake, surrounded by plane trees. The shaded pathways and the cool waters make it a popular spot for a tranquil retreat from the summer heat.

Off-the-Beaten-Path Villages:

Beyond the well-known tourist destinations, the inland beauty of Rhodes is best explored through its charming villages. Each village has its unique character, whether it's the stone houses of Embonas, the traditional architecture of Eleousa, or the medieval charm of Monolithos.

Venturing into the inland beauty of Rhodes unveils a side of the island that often goes unnoticed. The mountains and valleys, steeped in history and natural wonders, invite you to escape the coastal bustle and embrace the tranquility and authenticity that define the heart of Rhodes.

Exploring Rhodes' Diverse Landscapes

Rhodes, beyond its historical and cultural richness, is a canvas painted with diverse landscapes that captivate the senses. This chapter invites you on a journey through the varied terrains that define the island's natural beauty.

Golden Beaches and Turquoise Waters:

The coastal allure of Rhodes is synonymous with its golden beaches and crystal-clear waters. From the popular shores of Faliraki and Tsambika to the secluded beauty of Anthony Quinn Bay, the island's beaches offer a spectrum of experiences, whether you seek vibrant beach life, water sports, or tranquil relaxation.

Rocky Shores and Hidden Coves:

Beyond the well-known beaches, Rhodes boasts rocky shores and hidden coves waiting to be discovered. Ladiko Bay, with its rugged cliffs and emerald-green waters, and Traganou Beach, adorned with caves and crystal-clear sea, invite those who seek a more secluded coastal escape.

Prassonisi Peninsula: Where Seas Converge:

At the southern tip of Rhodes, the Prassonisi Peninsula offers a unique spectacle where the Aegean and Mediterranean Seas converge. This wind-swept paradise is a haven for windsurfers and kitesurfers, providing an adrenaline-packed coastal experience against a backdrop of natural beauty.

Petaloudes (Butterfly Valley): A Lush Sanctuary:

Butterfly Valley, or Petaloudes, is a verdant sanctuary nestled in the mountains. During the summer months, thousands of Jersey Tiger moths create a colorful display. The valley's lush greenery, streams, and waterfalls contribute to a serene ambiance, making it a must-visit for nature enthusiasts.

Mount Attavyros: The Island's Rooftop:

Rising to a height of approximately 1,215 meters, Mount Attavyros stands as the rooftop of Rhodes. The ascent through changing ecosystems, from olive groves to pine forests, rewards hikers with panoramic views of the island and the surrounding seas, offering a glimpse of Rhodes from a different perspective.

Valleys of Abundant Agriculture:

Rhodes' inland beauty is enriched by valleys that serve as fertile grounds for agriculture. Olive groves, vineyards, and orchards carpet the valleys, contributing to the island's agricultural abundance. The cultivation of olives, grapes, and other produce is not only a scenic sight but also an integral part of Rhodes' cultural and culinary heritage.

Seven Springs (Epta Piges): A Refreshing Oasis:

Tucked away in a wooded area, the Seven Springs is a refreshing oasis in the midst of the mountains. Natural springs converge to form a small lake, surrounded by plane trees. The shaded pathways and the cool waters make it a popular spot for a tranquil retreat from the summer heat.

Inland Villages: Timeless Charm and Hospitality:

The inland villages of Rhodes offer a glimpse into traditional island life. Embonas, known for its vineyards and wine production, Eleousa with its traditional architecture, and Monolithos with its medieval charm are just a few examples of villages where time seems to stand still, and hospitality is a way of life.

Exploring Rhodes' diverse landscapes is like flipping through the pages of a nature lover's dream. From the turquoise waters of its beaches to the lush greenery of its mountains, the island invites you to discover the harmonious interplay of nature's elements that make Rhodes a destination of unparalleled beauty.

Chapter 4

Cultural Mosaic of Rhodes

Local Traditions and Festivals: Celebrating the Soul of Rhodes

Rhodes, with its rich cultural tapestry, is a living mosaic of traditions and festivities that reflect the island's deep-rooted heritage. This section unveils the vibrant spectrum of local traditions and festivals that add a dynamic and celebratory layer to Rhodes' cultural identity.

Panigiria: Traditional Village Festivals:

The heart of Rhodes beats in its villages, where traditional Panigiria (festivals) come alive. These celebrations are woven into the fabric of rural life, featuring lively music, traditional dances, and local delicacies. Villagers and visitors alike join in the festivities, creating an atmosphere of communal joy and unity.

Apokries: Carnival Season Extravaganza:

Apokries marks the Carnival season in Rhodes, bringing a burst of color and revelry to the island. Festivities include elaborate parades, vibrant costumes, and music echoing through the streets. The highlight is the Grand Carnival Parade in Rhodes Town, where locals and tourists gather to witness the exuberant spectacle.

Easter Celebrations: A Time of Reflection and Joy:

Easter holds a special place in the hearts of the Rhodians, marked by a unique blend of religious ceremonies and festive traditions. The Resurrection service, the midnight procession, and the traditional cracking of red-dyed eggs create an atmosphere of both solemnity and joy, bringing communities together.

Medieval Rose Festival: A Journey to the Past:

The Medieval Rose Festival in Rhodes Town transports visitors to the island's medieval heyday. This cultural event celebrates the island's history with reenactments, parades, and theatrical performances. The medieval streets become a stage for knights, minstrels, and artisans, offering a captivating journey back in time.

Klidonas Festival: A Midsummer Night's Celebration:

Klidonas, celebrated on the night of June 23rd, marks the summer solstice. Traditionally associated with love and fertility, the festival involves the burning of bonfires, dancing, and rituals to ward off evil spirits. It is a night of merriment and ancient customs that showcase the island's connection to its pagan past.

Wine Festivals: A Toast to Tradition:

Rhodes, known for its vineyards and wine production, hosts vibrant wine festivals. These celebrations of Dionysian spirit feature wine tastings, traditional dances, and local music. Embonas, the wine-producing village, is particularly renowned for its lively wine festival that attracts both locals and wine enthusiasts.

Saints' Feast Days: Religious and Cultural Blend:

The feast days of saints hold both religious significance and cultural celebrations. Villages across the island honor their patron saints with processions, church services, and communal gatherings. These events provide a glimpse into the fusion of religious devotion and cultural expression that defines Rhodes' identity.

Music and Dance: Rhodian Rhythms:

Music and dance are integral to the cultural mosaic of Rhodes. Traditional Rhodian music, often accompanied by instruments like the lyra and laouto, sets the stage for lively dances. The expressive movements of the Sousta and Kalamatianos reflect the island's rich dance heritage, inviting everyone to join in the rhythmic celebration.

As you delve into the local traditions and festivals of Rhodes, you'll witness a vibrant expression of the island's soul. The blending of ancient rituals with modern celebrations creates a cultural mosaic that invites you to not just observe but actively participate in the lively spirit of Rhodes.

Arts and Crafts: A Glimpse into Rhodes' Creative Scene

Rhodes, beyond its historical and natural splendors, is a canvas for artistic expression and craftsmanship. This section offers a detailed exploration of the island's arts and crafts scene, where tradition meets innovation, and creativity finds its home.

Traditional Pottery: Artistry in Clay:

The art of pottery in Rhodes is a testament to the island's rich cultural heritage. Skilled artisans mold clay into intricate designs, creating a range of functional and decorative items. Traditional motifs, often inspired by nature and mythology, adorn plates, vases, and other ceramics, offering unique pieces that capture the essence of Rhodes.

Iconography: Sacred Artistry:

Rhodes has a long-standing tradition of iconography, a form of sacred art that involves painting religious icons. Skilled iconographers use ancient techniques to create images of saints and religious figures. These works of art can be found in churches and monasteries across the island, showcasing the spiritual and artistic dimensions of Rhodes' heritage.

Embroidery: Threaded Tales:

Embroidery is a cherished craft in Rhodes, passed down through generations. Intricate patterns and vibrant colors characterize traditional Rhodian embroidery. Local women skillfully weave stories into fabric, creating garments and textiles that reflect the island's cultural identity. You can find these handmade treasures in local markets and shops.

Ceramic and Mosaic Art: A Colorful Legacy:

Rhodes' historic connection to ancient civilizations is reflected in its ceramic and mosaic art. From intricate floor mosaics in archaeological sites to contemporary ceramic creations, the island continues to celebrate this colorful legacy. Artisans fuse traditional techniques with modern designs, producing pieces that capture the spirit of Rhodes.

Woodcarving: Crafting with Precision:

Woodcarving is a craft that thrives in Rhodes, with artisans meticulously shaping wood into intricate designs. From furniture to decorative items, the precision and skill displayed in Rhodian woodcarving highlight a dedication to preserving traditional craftsmanship while adapting to modern tastes.

Rhodian Jewelry: Adornments with History:

The art of jewelry-making in Rhodes is steeped in history. Skilled craftsmen create intricate pieces inspired by ancient Greek and Byzantine designs. Symbols of the island, such as the rose, are often incorporated into these wearable works of art, making Rhodian jewelry a unique and meaningful adornment.

Contemporary Art Scene: A Modern Expression:

Rhodes' artistic scene is not confined to tradition; it also embraces contemporary expressions. Galleries and studios across the island showcase the works of modern artists who draw inspiration from the landscapes, history, and cultural diversity of Rhodes. From paintings to sculptures, the contemporary art scene reflects the evolving identity of the island.

Artisanal Markets and Workshops: Hands-On Experience:

Travelers seeking a deeper connection to Rhodes' creative scene can explore artisanal markets and workshops. These spaces provide an opportunity to meet local artists, witness the crafting process firsthand, and even try your hand at creating your own piece of Rhodian art.

As you delve into Rhodes' arts and crafts scene, you'll discover a world where heritage and innovation converge. From the intricate details of traditional crafts to the vibrant expressions of contemporary art, the island invites you to explore the creative spirit that adds another layer to its cultural mosaic.

Museums: Unveiling the Tapestry of History and Culture

Rhodes, with its rich history and diverse cultural influences, is home to a captivating array of museums that invite you to step back in time and explore the island's multifaceted heritage. From archaeological wonders to medieval treasures, each museum unravels a unique chapter in Rhodes' story.

Archaeological Museum of Rhodes: A Journey Through Antiquity:

Located in Rhodes Town, the Archaeological Museum is a treasure trove of artifacts that span the island's ancient history. Exhibits include sculptures, pottery, and artifacts from various archaeological sites on Rhodes, offering a comprehensive overview of the island's role in the ancient world. Highlights include pieces from the classical, Hellenistic, and Roman periods.

Palace of the Grand Master of the Knights of Rhodes: Living History:

While not a traditional museum, the Palace of the Grand Master in Rhodes Town serves as a captivating showcase of medieval history. Explore the grand halls, courtyards, and chambers that once housed the Grand Master of the Knights of Rhodes. The palace also features an exhibition on the history of the Knights Hospitaller and the medieval period on the island.

Folk Art Museum (Museum of Decorative Arts): Craftsmanship and Tradition:

Housed in a historic mansion in Rhodes Town, the Folk Art Museum celebrates the island's traditional crafts and decorative arts. The collection includes intricate embroidery, traditional costumes, and handcrafted items that provide insight into the daily life and craftsmanship of the Rhodian people.

Rhodes Jewish Museum: Preserving a Heritage:

Located in the Jewish Quarter of Rhodes Town, the Rhodes Jewish Museum tells the story of the island's once-vibrant Jewish community. Exhibits showcase the history, culture, and traditions of the Jewish people on Rhodes, offering a poignant glimpse into a community that flourished for centuries.

Museum of Modern Greek Art: Contemporary Expressions:

Situated in the Medieval City of Rhodes, the Museum of Modern Greek Art features a collection of paintings, sculptures, and installations by Greek artists from the 20th century to the present. The museum provides a platform for contemporary artistic expression, showcasing the evolving cultural landscape of Greece.

Art Galleries: A Canvas of Expression

Beyond the realm of museums, Rhodes boasts a vibrant art scene with galleries that showcase a diverse range of artistic expressions. From traditional works to contemporary creations, these galleries offer a glimpse into the evolving identity of Rhodes through the eyes of its artists.

Art Gallery of the Municipality of Rhodes: Local and International Perspectives:

Located in Rhodes Town, the Art Gallery of the Municipality of Rhodes features rotating exhibitions that span a wide range of artistic styles and mediums. The gallery serves as a platform for both local and international artists, providing a dynamic space for creative exploration.

Contemporary Art Gallery: Cutting-Edge Creations:

The Contemporary Art Gallery, situated in Rhodes Town, focuses on showcasing cutting-edge contemporary art. The gallery exhibits works by emerging and established artists, offering visitors a chance to engage with the evolving trends and expressions within the art world.

Byzantine Museum of Rhodes: Icons and Religious Art:

While primarily focused on Byzantine religious art, the Byzantine Museum in Rhodes Town is also a gallery of sorts. The museum houses a collection of icons, religious artifacts, and frescoes, providing insight into the religious and artistic heritage of Rhodes during the Byzantine period.

Lindos Art Gallery: Coastal Inspirations:

The Lindos Art Gallery, located in the scenic village of Lindos, showcases works inspired by the natural beauty and cultural richness of Rhodes. The gallery often features paintings, sculptures, and crafts created by local artists, capturing the essence of Lindos and its surroundings.

Artistic Village Contemporary Art Gallery: Rural Inspirations:

Nestled in the countryside near Archangelos, the Artistic Village Contemporary Art Gallery combines art with the tranquility of rural Rhodes. The gallery features works by local and international artists, often drawing inspiration from the pastoral landscapes and cultural traditions of the island.

Exploring the museums and art galleries of Rhodes offers a nuanced understanding of the island's cultural heritage and artistic vitality. From ancient artifacts to contemporary creations, each venue contributes to the mosaic of experiences that make Rhodes a captivating destination for cultural enthusiasts.

Modern Influences on Traditional Culture

Rhodes, with its deep-rooted traditions, has not remained untouched by the currents of modernity. This section explores the dynamic fusion of modern influences with the island's traditional culture, creating a vibrant and evolving tapestry that reflects the resilience and adaptability of Rhodes' identity.

Contemporary Architecture: Bridging the Past and Present:

Modern influences on Rhodes' architecture are evident in the juxtaposition of contemporary structures against the backdrop of ancient and medieval buildings. The island's towns and villages showcase a blend of traditional aesthetics and modern design, creating a harmonious coexistence of the old and the new.

Culinary Innovations: A Modern Twist on Tradition:

Rhodes' culinary scene, rooted in traditional Greek and Mediterranean flavors, has embraced modern influences. Chefs and restaurateurs experiment with innovative techniques and global culinary trends, offering a fusion of traditional recipes with contemporary twists. This culinary evolution adds a dynamic flavor to the island's gastronomic identity.

Music and Entertainment: Modern Rhythms Meet Tradition:

The vibrant music scene of Rhodes harmonizes traditional Rhodian melodies with modern genres. Local musicians experiment with new sounds, blending traditional instruments with contemporary beats. From traditional folk music to modern interpretations, the island resonates with a diverse musical tapestry.

Artistic Expression: Modern Art Meets Ancient Inspiration:

Rhodes' art scene reflects a fusion of ancient inspiration and modern creativity. Contemporary artists draw on the island's rich history and natural beauty to create works that bridge the gap between tradition and innovation. Galleries and public spaces become platforms for the dialogue between the past and the present.

Fashion and Design: Traditional Roots in Modern Styles:

Rhodes' fashion and design industry showcase a balance between traditional craftsmanship and modern styles. Local designers often incorporate traditional patterns, textiles, and techniques into contemporary clothing and accessories. This synthesis of the old and the new is not only a reflection of style but also a celebration of cultural heritage.

Festivals and Events: Modern Celebrations with Ancient Roots:

Modern festivals and events in Rhodes often reinterpret ancient traditions, infusing them with contemporary elements. Whether it's a cultural festival, a music event, or a celebration of local produce, these gatherings provide a platform for both traditional and modern expressions, fostering a sense of community and inclusivity.

Education and Technology: Nurturing Innovation:

The education landscape of Rhodes has embraced modern methods and technologies while preserving a commitment to traditional knowledge. Educational institutions on the island strive to integrate the best of both worlds, preparing students to navigate a globalized world while grounding them in the cultural richness of Rhodes.

Tourism: Cultural Exchange in the Modern Era:

Tourism, a significant aspect of modern Rhodes, brings a continuous exchange of cultures. Visitors from around the world contribute to the island's cultural diversity, while also being introduced to the rich traditions and history of Rhodes. This interplay between locals and visitors adds a modern layer to the cultural narrative.

As Rhodes evolves in the modern era, the island's traditional culture remains a resilient foundation, adapting to and integrating with contemporary influences. The dynamic fusion of old and new creates a unique and ever-evolving identity that invites exploration and appreciation for the multifaceted nature of Rhodes' cultural mosaic.

Chapter 5

Rhodes Cuisine: A Gastronomic Journey

Savory Delights: Culinary Traditions

Embark on a culinary odyssey through the rich tapestry of Rhodes' gastronomy, where age-old traditions and local ingredients come together to create a feast for the senses. From ancient flavors to modern interpretations, Rhodes' cuisine reflects the island's cultural heritage and a deep connection to the bountiful land and sea.

Olive Oil: Liquid Gold of Rhodes:

Central to Rhodian cuisine is the use of olive oil, often referred to as the "liquid gold" of the island. The fertile soil and abundant sunshine produce olives of exceptional quality, resulting in a rich and flavorful olive oil. Locals drizzle it generously over salads, grilled meats, and vegetables, imparting a distinct Mediterranean essence to their dishes.

Fresh Seafood: Gifts from the Aegean:

The island's proximity to the Aegean Sea ensures a bounty of fresh seafood gracing Rhodian tables. From grilled octopus and calamari to succulent fish dishes, the culinary tradition of Rhodes celebrates the fruits of the sea. Seafood tavernas along the coastline offer an authentic experience, allowing diners to savor the catch of the day.

Mezedes: Small Bites, Big Flavors:

Mezedes, small and shareable plates, are a cornerstone of Rhodian dining. These appetizers showcase the diversity of flavors and textures in the island's cuisine. From tzatziki, a yogurt and cucumber dip, to dolmades, grape leaves stuffed with rice and herbs, mezedes offer a delightful journey through the tastes of Rhodes.

Pitaroudia: A Savory Delight from the Fields:

Pitaroudia, a traditional Rhodian dish, encapsulates the essence of rural life. These savory fritters are made from chickpeas or fava beans, mixed with local herbs, and fried to golden perfection. Served with a squeeze of lemon, pitaroudia are a delicious example of the island's simple yet flavorful fare.

Lahanodolmades: Cabbage Rolls with a Twist:

Lahanodolmades, cabbage rolls stuffed with a flavorful mixture of rice, pine nuts, and herbs, showcase the influence of Ottoman cuisine on Rhodes. Often served with a dollop of yogurt, these rolls are a testament to the island's cultural diversity and the fusion of culinary traditions over the centuries.

Koulouria: Sweet and Savory Sesame Rings:

Koulouria are traditional sesame rings that straddle the line between sweet and savory. These baked delights, often enjoyed with a sprinkle of sesame seeds, offer a satisfying crunch and are perfect accompaniments to coffee or as a light snack. They represent the simple pleasures embedded in Rhodian culinary traditions.

Ladokouloura: Olive Oil Cookies:

Ladokouloura, olive oil cookies, are a sweet treat with a connection to the island's olive oil production. Made with a generous amount of olive oil, these cookies are soft and crumbly, offering a delightful taste of the Mediterranean. They are often flavored with orange zest or cinnamon, adding layers of aroma to this beloved dessert.

Rhodian Cheese: From the Pastures to the Plate:

The pastoral landscapes of Rhodes contribute to the production of exceptional local cheeses. Feta, mizithra, and graviera are among the varieties that find their way into salads, mezedes, and pastries. These cheeses, crafted with care and tradition, add richness and depth to Rhodian culinary creations.

Mastiha: A Unique Flavor from the Island:

Mastiha, a resin obtained from the mastic tree, is a unique ingredient that imparts a distinctive flavor to Rhodian desserts. From mastiha-flavored loukoum (Turkish delight) to ice cream and liqueurs, this aromatic resin adds a touch of exoticism to the island's sweet offerings.

Traditional Rhodian Wines: A Toast to Terroir:

The vineyards of Rhodes produce wines that reflect the island's terroir. From crisp whites to robust reds, Rhodian wines complement the local cuisine. Embonas, known for its wine production, invites visitors to explore the vineyards and savor the flavors of Rhodian terroir in a glass.

As you indulge in the savory delights of Rhodian cuisine, you embark on a culinary journey that intertwines history, culture, and the bounty of land and sea. Each dish tells a story, and each flavor is a celebration of the island's gastronomic heritage.

Must-Try Dishes and Local Specialties

Rhodes' culinary landscape is a treasure trove of flavors, featuring a myriad of must-try dishes and local specialties that showcase the island's culinary prowess. Prepare your taste buds for a delightful journey through Rhodian gastronomy.

Souvlaki: Grilled Perfection:

Souvlaki, skewered and grilled meat, is a ubiquitous delight in Rhodes. Whether it's succulent lamb, chicken, or pork, the meat is marinated in aromatic herbs and spices before being charred to perfection. Served with pita bread and a side of tzatziki, souvlaki is a quintessential taste of Greece.

Moussaka: Layers of Flavor:

Moussaka is a savory casserole that layers eggplant, minced meat, and béchamel sauce. Baked to golden perfection, this hearty dish combines the earthiness of eggplant with the richness of meat and the creamy elegance of béchamel. It's a comforting and flavorful centerpiece of Rhodian cuisine.

Pitaroudia: Chickpea Fritters:

Pitaroudia, savory fritters made from chickpeas, fava beans, or a combination of both, are a delightful street food and meze option. Mixed with local herbs and fried until golden, these crispy bites offer a taste of Rhodian simplicity and flavor.

Lavraki Psito: Grilled Sea Bass:

Lavraki Psito, or grilled sea bass, epitomizes the island's celebration of fresh seafood. Seasoned with olive oil, lemon, and herbs, the sea bass is expertly grilled to retain its natural flavors.

Served with a side of Greek salad, it's a culinary ode to the Aegean's bounty.

Gemista: Stuffed Vegetables:

Gemista, meaning "filled" in Greek, refers to vegetables stuffed with a delicious mixture of rice, pine nuts, and herbs. Tomatoes, bell peppers, and zucchini are commonly used as vessels for this delectable filling. Baked until tender, gemista is a flavorful vegetarian delight.

Kleftiko: Slow-Cooked Lamb:

Kleftiko is a traditional slow-cooked lamb dish, a testament to the island's pastoral heritage. The lamb is marinated with garlic, lemon, and local herbs before being wrapped in parchment paper and slow-cooked to tender perfection. The result is a melt-in-your-mouth culinary experience.

Pastitsio: Baked Pasta Delight:

Pastitsio is a baked pasta dish that layers tube-shaped pasta with a rich meat sauce and béchamel topping. The flavors meld together in the oven, creating a satisfying and comforting dish. It's a classic example of Rhodian comfort food.

Baklava: Sweet Layers of Joy:

Baklava, a dessert made of layers of filo pastry, chopped nuts, and honey or syrup, is a sweet finale to a Rhodian meal. The combination of crisp layers and sweet, nutty filling creates a delightful contrast of textures. Served in small, irresistible portions, baklava is a sweet symphony for the taste buds.

Loukoumades: Golden Honey Balls:

Loukoumades are deep-fried dough balls, crispy on the outside and fluffy on the inside. After frying, they are drizzled with honey, sprinkled with cinnamon or sesame seeds, and sometimes topped with chopped nuts. These golden spheres of sweetness are a popular indulgence in Rhodian desserts.

Sikomaida: Fig Delight:

Sikomaida is a traditional Rhodian sweet made from dried figs, almonds, and honey. The dried figs are stuffed with almonds and then dipped in honey, creating a chewy, sweet, and nutty treat. Sikomaida is not only a delicious dessert but also a nod to the island's abundance of figs.

Rhodian Wines: A Taste of Terroir:

Don't miss the opportunity to savor the local wines of Rhodes. From the robust reds of Embonas to the crisp whites produced across the island, Rhodian wines offer a nuanced experience that complements the diverse flavors of the local cuisine.

Each of these must-try dishes and local specialties is a culinary work of art, a manifestation of Rhodes' rich culinary heritage, and an invitation to savor the unique flavors that define the island's gastronomic identity. Bon appétit!

Hidden Gems for Food Enthusiasts: Culinary Discoveries Off the Beaten Path

For the discerning food enthusiast seeking culinary adventures beyond the well-trodden paths, Rhodes reveals hidden gems that promise an authentic and unforgettable gastronomic experience. Venture off the beaten path and explore these culinary treasures tucked away in the heart of the island.

Taverna Kostas: A Local Favorite in Afandou:

Located in the charming village of Afandou, Taverna Kostas is a hidden gem celebrated by locals. This family-run taverna offers a warm and welcoming atmosphere, where traditional recipes are prepared with a touch of personal flair. Indulge in their lamb dishes, grilled to perfection, and savor the flavors of authentic Rhodian hospitality.

To Steno: Gastronomic Delights in the Old Town:

Nestled in the narrow alleys of Rhodes Town's Old Town, To Steno is a culinary oasis for those seeking a refined and intimate dining experience. The menu showcases a fusion of traditional Rhodian flavors with modern culinary techniques. Each dish is a masterpiece, and the ambiance transports diners to a bygone era.

Koukos Taverna: Seafood Paradise in Kiotari:

Perched on the shores of Kiotari, Koukos Taverna is a seafood haven that often escapes the tourist radar. Feast on freshly caught fish and seafood while enjoying panoramic views of the Aegean Sea. The simple yet elegant setting allows the flavors of the sea to take center stage, making it a must-visit for seafood enthusiasts.

To Marouli: Vegetarian Delights in Archangelos:

To Marouli, located in the picturesque village of Archangelos, is a haven for vegetarian food enthusiasts. The menu features a creative array of dishes crafted from locally sourced vegetables and herbs. From stuffed grape leaves to inventive salads, To Marouli proves that Rhodian cuisine extends its warm welcome to vegetarians.

Agalma: Artful Dining in Lindos:

Tucked away in the enchanting village of Lindos, Agalma is a culinary gem that seamlessly blends art and gastronomy. The menu is a canvas of carefully curated dishes, each presented as a work of art. The fusion of flavors and the elegant setting make Agalma a destination for those seeking a dining experience that transcends the ordinary.

To Limeri: Traditional Flavors in Malona:

To Limeri, situated in the serene village of Malona, is a hidden culinary gem preserving the authenticity of Rhodian flavors. This taverna, embraced by locals, offers a menu steeped in tradition. From slow-cooked stews to handmade pastas, To Limeri invites food enthusiasts to savor the soulful essence of Rhodian home cooking.

Ouzokafenes: Ouzo and Meze in Embonas:

In the mountain village of Embonas, Ouzokafenes is a delightful spot where ouzo flows freely, and meze plates abound. This traditional ouzeri captures the convivial spirit of Rhodian gatherings. Sip on ouzo, nibble on mezedes, and immerse yourself in the lively atmosphere that defines this hidden gem.

Ktima Fasouli: Wine and Gastronomy in Pastida:

Wine enthusiasts and food connoisseurs will find delight in Ktima Fasouli, a winery and restaurant in the village of Pastida. Set amidst vineyards, this hidden gem offers not only a variety of local wines but also a culinary journey through Rhodian specialties. The wine and dine experience in this tranquil setting is a testament to the island's terroir.

To Perasma: A Taste of Tradition in Salakos:

To Perasma, located in the village of Salakos, is a traditional taverna where time seems to stand still. The menu features recipes passed down through generations, offering a taste of Rhodian heritage. The ambiance, with its rustic charm, creates an immersive experience that transports diners to the heart of Rhodian tradition.

Oinomageiremata: Wine and Gastronomy in the New Town:

In Rhodes Town's New Town, Oinomageiremata is a hidden gem that marries wine and gastronomy with flair. The menu, a fusion of Greek and Mediterranean influences, complements an extensive wine list. The contemporary setting and culinary artistry make Oinomageiremata a modern enclave for those seeking refined dining experiences.

Discovering these hidden gems for food enthusiasts in Rhodes is not just a journey through flavors but a cultural exploration. Each establishment captures the essence of Rhodian cuisine in its own unique way, inviting you to savor the culinary secrets that the island holds beyond the well-traveled routes.

Chapter 6

Transportation Options

Getting There

Embarking on your journey to Rhodes is the initial step in a thrilling adventure. The island is well-connected, and various transportation options cater to different preferences and travel styles. Whether you prefer the convenience of air travel or the scenic route by sea, here are the primary ways to reach the captivating island of Rhodes.

By Air: Rhodes International Airport "Diagoras" (RHO):

Convenient and Direct: The most common way to reach Rhodes is by air. The island is served by Rhodes International Airport, also known as Diagoras Airport. The airport is well-connected to major cities in Europe and beyond, making it a convenient gateway to the island.

- Direct Flights: Numerous airlines operate direct flights to Rhodes, particularly during the tourist season. Direct flights are available from major European cities, including Athens, London, Berlin, and Amsterdam, among others.
- Flight Duration: The flight duration varies depending on the departure location. Flights from European cities typically range from 2 to 4 hours, providing a relatively quick and efficient way to reach the island.

By Sea: Ferries and Cruise Ships:

- Scenic Sea Routes: For those seeking a more leisurely and scenic approach, traveling to Rhodes by sea is an enticing option. Ferries and cruise ships connect Rhodes to various ports in Greece and neighboring countries.

- Ferry Services: Regular ferry services operate between Rhodes and mainland Greece, including the ports of Piraeus and Thessaloniki. Additionally, there are ferry connections to other Greek islands, such as Crete, Kos, and Symi.

- Cruise Ships: Rhodes is a popular port of call for cruise ships in the Mediterranean. Cruise enthusiasts can enjoy the experience of arriving at the island's historic harbor, surrounded by medieval walls and the imposing Palace of the Grand Master.

Combination of Air and Sea: Island Hopping:

- Explore the Aegean Islands: If you're planning to explore multiple Greek islands, island hopping is a fantastic option. Begin your journey by flying into Athens or another major hub, then continue your adventure by taking ferries to Rhodes and other islands of your choice.

- Flexibility of Itineraries: Island hopping allows you to customize your itinerary, discovering the unique charm of each island. It's an ideal option for travelers who relish the freedom to explore diverse landscapes and cultures.

Choosing how to get to Rhodes depends on your preferences, travel itinerary, and the type of experience you seek. Whether you opt for the convenience of air travel or the scenic route by sea, your journey to Rhodes marks the beginning of an exploration into the history, culture, and natural beauty that the island has to offer.

Getting Around

Once you've arrived in Rhodes, getting around the island is a crucial aspect of maximizing your exploration. Rhodes offers diverse transportation options to suit various preferences and travel styles. Whether you prefer the freedom of your own vehicle or the convenience of public transport, here are the primary ways to navigate the captivating island.

Car Rentals: Explore at Your Own Pace:

- Convenience and Flexibility: Renting a car is a popular choice for exploring Rhodes independently. Numerous car rental agencies operate on the island, offering a variety of vehicles to suit different needs.
- Scenic Drives: Rhodes boasts well-maintained roads that connect major towns, archaeological sites, and picturesque villages. A rental car provides the flexibility to embark on scenic drives, discover hidden gems, and take detours off the beaten path.

Public Buses: Budget-Friendly Exploration:

- Extensive Network: Rhodes has an extensive public bus network that connects major towns and popular tourist destinations. The central bus station in Rhodes Town serves as a hub for routes spanning the island.
- Affordable Option: Public buses are a budget-friendly option for travelers looking to explore the major attractions without the hassle of driving. Bus schedules are accessible, and routes cover a wide range of destinations.

Taxis: Convenient and Accessible:

- Door-to-Door Service: Taxis are readily available in Rhodes Town and major tourist areas. They provide a convenient and efficient means of transportation, especially for shorter trips or when you prefer a comfortable and direct transfer to your destination.
- Fares and Negotiation: It's advisable to confirm the fare with the driver before starting your journey. While taxi fares are regulated, it's a good practice to ensure clarity to avoid misunderstandings.

Scooter and Motorcycle Rentals: Nimble and Adventurous:

- Explore Narrow Streets: For those seeking a nimble and adventurous mode of transportation, renting a scooter or motorcycle is a popular choice. This option allows you to navigate narrow streets and reach more secluded spots.
- Rental Services: Rental services for scooters and motorcycles can be found in tourist hubs, providing a thrilling way to explore the island with the wind in your hair.

Bicycles: Eco-Friendly Exploration:

- Cycling Paths: Embrace the eco-friendly side of exploration by renting a bicycle. Rhodes offers a growing network of cycling paths, particularly in coastal areas. Biking allows you to enjoy the scenery at a leisurely pace and provides a unique perspective on the island's beauty.

Boat Tours: Island-Hopping Adventures:

- Sea Exploration: Given Rhodes' coastal allure, boat tours offer a delightful way to explore neighboring islands, hidden coves, and pristine beaches. Various boat excursions depart from Rhodes Town and other coastal towns, providing a unique perspective of the island from the sea.

Walking: Strolling Through History:

- Historic Exploration: Many of Rhodes' historic sites, especially in the Old Town, are best explored on foot. Walking allows you to immerse yourself in the charm of cobblestone streets, discover hidden alleys, and appreciate the intricate details of medieval architecture.

Understanding the diverse transportation options in Rhodes empowers you to tailor your exploration to your preferences and the destinations you wish to uncover. Whether you choose the freedom of a rental car, the convenience of public transport, or the adventure of two wheels, each mode of transportation adds a unique dimension to your journey across this captivating island.

Chapter 7

Accommodations Options

Choosing the right accommodation is a pivotal aspect of ensuring a comfortable and enjoyable stay on the island of Rhodes. The diversity of options caters to various preferences and budgets, allowing you to tailor your accommodation to the type of experience you seek. Here are insights into the accommodation landscape on Rhodes:

Hotels and Resorts: Comfort and Luxury

When it comes to hotels and resorts in Rhodes, the island offers a diverse range of options catering to various preferences. Whether you seek the luxurious comfort of a seaside resort, the historical charm of a hotel within Rhodes Town, or the convenience of an all-inclusive package, Rhodes has something to offer.

Seaside Resorts:

- **Amathus Beach Hotel Rhodes (Ixia):** Nestled along the coastline in Ixia, the Amathus Beach Hotel is a five-star resort offering an indulgent retreat. With spacious rooms, multiple swimming pools, private beach access, and gourmet dining options, this resort provides a luxurious escape.
- **Sheraton Rhodes Resort (Ialyssos):** Overlooking the Aegean Sea in Ialyssos, the Sheraton Rhodes Resort combines modern amenities with a stunning coastal setting. The resort features expansive gardens, a spa, multiple restaurants, and a private beach, making it an ideal choice for those seeking both comfort and convenience.

Historic Hotels in Rhodes Town:

- **Rodos Park Suites & Spa:** Situated near the medieval walls of Rhodes Town, Rodos Park Suites & Spa offers a blend of historical charm and contemporary luxury. The hotel features elegantly decorated rooms, a spa with indoor pool, and a rooftop restaurant with panoramic views.
- **Spirit Of The Knights Boutique Hotel:** Located within the medieval Old Town, this boutique hotel captures the essence of Rhodes' history. With uniquely designed rooms, a tranquil courtyard, and personalized service, it provides an intimate and atmospheric stay.

All-Inclusive Options:

- **Atlantica Imperial Resort (Kolymbia):** For those seeking an all-inclusive experience, the Atlantica Imperial Resort in Kolymbia is a notable choice. With a range of dining options, pools, sports facilities, and entertainment, this resort caters to families and couples alike.
- **Lindos Imperial Resort & Spa (Kiotari):** Situated on the southeast coast, the Lindos Imperial Resort & Spa offers an extensive all-inclusive package. With direct beach access, multiple pools, and various dining venues, it provides a comprehensive and luxurious holiday experience.

Practical Tips for Hotel and Resort Stays:

- Booking Timing: Secure your reservation well in advance, especially if you plan to visit during peak tourist seasons. This ensures availability and often more favorable rates.
- Location Considerations: Choose accommodations based on your preferred activities. Whether it's enjoying beachfront relaxation, exploring historical sites, or

venturing into the vibrant nightlife, consider the location that aligns with your interests.

- Reviews and Ratings: Utilize online platforms to read reviews and ratings from fellow travelers. Look for feedback on cleanliness, service quality, and the accuracy of amenities to make informed decisions.
- Special Offers and Packages: Explore special offers and packages provided by hotels and resorts. This may include early booking discounts, honeymoon packages, or spa and dining credits, adding value to your stay.

Selecting the right hotel or resort sets the tone for your Rhodes experience, whether you're seeking relaxation, historical immersion, or a blend of both. These recommended accommodations offer a glimpse into the diverse offerings on the island, ensuring a memorable and comfortable stay.

Villas and Vacation Rentals: Privacy and Flexibility

For those who prioritize privacy, independence, and a home-like atmosphere, Rhodes offers a variety of villas and vacation rentals. From secluded villas nestled in scenic landscapes to traditional houses in charming villages, these accommodations provide a unique and immersive experience.

Secluded Villas:

- **Villa Kallista (Kiotari):** Situated near Kiotari on the southeast coast, Villa Kallista offers a private and luxurious retreat. With stunning sea views, a private pool, and spacious interiors, this villa provides an idyllic setting for relaxation and tranquility.
- **Villa Amara (Lindos):** Overlooking the iconic Acropolis of Lindos, Villa Amara combines modern amenities with

traditional architecture. The villa features a rooftop terrace, a private courtyard, and easy access to the historic sites and beaches of Lindos.

Traditional Houses in Villages:

- **Archontiko Angelou (Emponas):** Located in the picturesque village of Emponas, Archontiko Angelou is a traditional guesthouse offering a charming stay. With stone-built rooms, a courtyard, and proximity to local tavernas, it provides a taste of authentic village life.
- **Petrino Cottage (Asklipio):** Nestled in the village of Asklipio, Petrino Cottage is a restored stone house with rustic charm. Surrounded by olive groves, the cottage offers a peaceful retreat while being close to historical sites such as the Castle of Asklipio.

Vacation Rentals:

- **Luxury Beachfront Apartment (Rhodes Town):** For those desiring a central location, this luxury beachfront apartment in Rhodes Town provides both convenience and style. With modern amenities, sea views, and proximity to the Old Town, it offers a comfortable urban retreat.
- **Traditional Lindian House (Lindos):** Immerse yourself in the charm of Lindos by staying in a traditional house near the Acropolis. This vacation rental combines authenticity with modern comforts, allowing you to experience the unique ambiance of Lindos.

Practical Tips for Villa and Vacation Rental Stays:

- Booking Platforms: Utilize reputable booking platforms such as Airbnb, Booking.com, or local agencies specializing in villa rentals. These platforms often provide detailed descriptions, reviews, and secure payment options.

- Amenities and Facilities: Review the amenities and facilities offered by each villa or vacation rental. Consider factors such as the presence of a kitchen, private pool, outdoor spaces, and proximity to local attractions.
- Communication with Hosts: Establish clear communication with the property owner or manager before your arrival. This ensures a smooth check-in process and allows you to address any specific requirements or questions you may have.
- Local Experiences: Seek recommendations from hosts on local experiences, hidden gems, and authentic eateries. Hosts often have valuable insights that enhance your overall stay and provide a deeper connection to the destination.

Choosing a villa or vacation rental in Rhodes allows you to create a personalized and immersive experience, whether you prefer the seclusion of a villa, the charm of a traditional house, or the convenience of a centrally located apartment. These recommended accommodations offer a glimpse into the diverse and enchanting options available on the island.

Boutique and Guesthouse Experiences: Personalized Hospitality

Rhodes is home to several boutique hotels and guesthouses that prioritize personalized service, unique design, and an intimate atmosphere. These accommodations, scattered across the island, offer a distinct character, reflecting both the owner's vision and the cultural richness of Rhodes.

Boutique Hotels:

- **Atrium Platinum Luxury Resort Hotel & Spa (Ixia):** Blending contemporary luxury with personalized service, Atrium Platinum is a five-star boutique hotel in Ixia. With spacious rooms, a spa, multiple dining options, and panoramic sea views, it provides an upscale and intimate retreat.

- **Elakati Luxury Boutique Hotel (Rhodes Town):** Located in the heart of Rhodes Town, Elakati Luxury Boutique Hotel offers a blend of historical charm and modern comfort. The hotel features elegantly designed rooms, a courtyard with a pool, and a rooftop terrace with views of the Old Town.

Charming Guesthouses:

- **Marco Polo Mansion (Rhodes Old Town):** Situated in the medieval Old Town of Rhodes, the Marco Polo Mansion is a charming guesthouse with a rich history. The rooms are adorned with antique furnishings, creating an ambiance that transports guests to another era.

- **Lindos Harmony Suites (Lindos):** In the scenic village of Lindos, Lindos Harmony Suites offers a boutique experience with a focus on tranquility. The suites are elegantly designed, and the property features a rooftop terrace with panoramic views of Lindos and the Acropolis.

Practical Tips for Boutique and Guesthouse Stays:

- Theme and Atmosphere: Consider the theme and atmosphere of the boutique hotel or guesthouse. Whether it's a historic mansion, a modern design, or a traditional setting, choose an accommodation that resonates with your preferences.

- Personalized Service: Boutique accommodations often excel in providing personalized service. Take advantage of this by communicating your preferences and expectations with the staff, allowing them to tailor your experience.
- Central vs. Secluded: Decide whether you prefer a central location for easy access to attractions and nightlife or a secluded setting for a more tranquil retreat. Boutique accommodations on Rhodes cater to both preferences.
- Local Experiences: Seek recommendations from the staff or owners on local experiences, dining, and off-the-beaten-path attractions. Boutique hotels and guesthouses are often well-connected to the local community and can offer valuable insights.

Choosing a boutique hotel or guesthouse in Rhodes allows you to experience the island with a touch of luxury and individuality. Whether you opt for the charm of a guesthouse in the Old Town or the contemporary elegance of a boutique hotel in Ixia, these recommended accommodations provide a unique and memorable stay on the island.

Budget-Friendly Stays: Affordable Exploration

Rhodes offers budget-friendly accommodation options for travelers seeking affordability without compromising comfort. From hostels and budget hotels to guesthouses in charming villages, these recommendations cater to those looking for cost-effective stays without sacrificing the essence of the island.

Hostels:

- **Stay Hostel Apartments (Rhodes Town):** Located in the heart of Rhodes Town, Stay Hostel Apartments provides budget-conscious travelers with a clean and vibrant atmosphere. The hostel offers dormitory-style and private rooms, making it suitable for solo travelers and small groups.
- **STAY Lindos Hostel (Lindos):** Embrace the laid-back atmosphere of Lindos at STAY Lindos Hostel. This budget-friendly option is situated in the heart of Lindos, offering dormitory and private rooms, as well as a communal kitchen for self-catering.

Budget Hotels:

- **Spot Hotel (Rhodes Town):** Conveniently located in Rhodes Town, Spot Hotel offers budget-friendly accommodation without compromising on comfort. The hotel provides simple yet cozy rooms and is within walking distance of the medieval Old Town.
- **Hotel Galaxias (Ixia):** For those seeking affordability in the Ixia area, Hotel Galaxias is a budget-friendly option. The hotel offers basic yet comfortable rooms and is situated close to the beach and various dining options.

Pension and Guesthouses:

- **Pension Nikos (Archangelos):** Immerse yourself in the local atmosphere of Archangelos at Pension Nikos. This budget-friendly guesthouse offers simple and clean rooms in a village setting, providing an authentic experience away from the tourist crowds.
- **Pansion Maria (Faliraki):** Located in the lively resort town of Faliraki, Pansion Maria is a budget-friendly option

with a family-friendly atmosphere. The guesthouse offers basic rooms and is within walking distance of the beach and entertainment venues.

Practical Tips for Budget-Friendly Stays:

- Advance Booking: Secure your accommodation in advance, especially during peak tourist seasons. Booking early often results in more affordable rates.
- Flexible Dates: If possible, consider traveling during the shoulder seasons when prices may be lower, and there are fewer tourists.
- Local Transportation: Choose accommodations near public transportation hubs for budget-friendly and convenient travel around the island.
- Self-Catering Options: Look for accommodations with kitchen facilities or communal kitchens to save on dining expenses by preparing your meals.

Choosing budget-friendly stays on Rhodes allows you to allocate more resources for exploring the island's attractions, trying local cuisine, and engaging in various activities. Whether you opt for a hostel in Rhodes Town, a budget hotel in Ixia, or a guesthouse in a charming village, these recommendations provide cost-effective options for a memorable stay on the island.

Selecting the right accommodation enhances your overall experience on Rhodes, allowing you to tailor your stay to your preferences and immerse yourself in the unique character of the island. Whether you opt for the comfort of a resort, the privacy of a villa, or the charm of a boutique hotel, Rhodes offers a diverse array of choices for every traveler.

Chapter 8

Outdoor Adventures and Recreation

Beach Escapes: Sun, Sand, and Serenity

Rhodes, with its extensive coastline, offers an array of pristine beaches where sun, sand, and serenity converge. Whether you seek a tranquil retreat, water sports excitement, or vibrant beachfront ambiance, the island caters to every beach lover's desires.

Lindos Beach (Lindos):

- Highlights: Nestled beneath the iconic Acropolis of Lindos, Lindos Beach is a postcard-perfect destination. The soft golden sand and crystal-clear waters create a serene setting, ideal for sunbathing and swimming.
- Water Activities: Lindos Beach provides opportunities for water sports enthusiasts. From paddleboarding to jet skiing, the turquoise waters offer a playground for those seeking an adrenaline rush.

Tsambika Beach (Tsambika):

- Highlights: Tsambika Beach, with its fine golden sand, is framed by imposing cliffs and lush vegetation. The shallow waters make it a family-friendly destination, while the panoramic views from the hilltop Tsambika Monastery add a touch of cultural charm.
- Adventure Option: For the adventurous, climb the steps to Tsambika Monastery for breathtaking views of the beach and surrounding landscapes.

Anthony Quinn Bay (Faliraki):

- Highlights: Named after the famous actor who starred in "The Guns of Navarone," Anthony Quinn Bay is a hidden gem with emerald-green waters and rugged surroundings. Snorkeling enthusiasts will find an underwater paradise, teeming with marine life.
- Scenic Trails: Explore the coastal trails around Anthony Quinn Bay for panoramic vistas and photo opportunities. The contrasting colors of the sea against the rocky landscape create a stunning backdrop.

Prasonisi Beach (Prasonisi):

- Highlights: Prasonisi Beach is a unique spot where the Aegean and Mediterranean seas meet, creating a narrow sandy isthmus. It's a paradise for windsurfers and kiteboarders, attracting enthusiasts from around the world.
- Windsurfing and Kitesurfing: Prasonisi's strong winds make it an ideal destination for windsurfing and kitesurfing. Whether you're a seasoned pro or a beginner, the conditions cater to all skill levels.

Agathi Beach (Haraki):

- Highlights: Agathi Beach is a tranquil haven with soft pebble shores and azure waters. The calm atmosphere and scenic surroundings make it perfect for a relaxing day by the sea.
- Tavernas and Beach Bars: Enjoy traditional Greek cuisine at the seaside tavernas or sip a refreshing drink at the beach bars. Agathi Beach provides a peaceful escape with the conveniences of local hospitality.

Practical Tips for Beach Escapes:

- Sun Protection: Bring sunscreen, hats, and sunglasses to protect yourself from the sun's intensity, especially during peak hours.
- Water Shoes: Consider bringing water shoes, especially for beaches with pebbles or rocky areas, to enhance your comfort when entering the water.
- Snorkeling Gear: If you enjoy snorkeling, bring your gear to explore the underwater beauty, especially in bays known for their rich marine life.
- Beach Exploration: Venture beyond the popular beaches to discover hidden coves and secluded spots, offering a more intimate connection with Rhodes' coastal beauty.

Rhodes' beaches are not just places to soak up the sun; they are gateways to diverse experiences, from water adventures to serene relaxation. Whether you're drawn to the lively shores of Faliraki or the secluded beauty of Agathi Beach, the island's coastline promises a beach escape tailored to your preferences

Hiking Trails and Nature Exploration

Rhodes, with its diverse landscapes and rich natural beauty, invites outdoor enthusiasts to explore its hiking trails and immerse themselves in the island's unique flora and fauna. From ancient paths leading to historic sites to trails winding through lush valleys, Rhodes offers a myriad of opportunities for nature lovers and hikers.

Valley of the Butterflies (Petaloudes):

- Highlights: The Valley of the Butterflies is a unique natural reserve where thousands of butterflies, particularly the

Jersey Tiger Moth, gather during the summer months. The picturesque valley, surrounded by plane and oriental sweetgum trees, creates a serene atmosphere.

- Butterfly Season: Visit during the butterfly season (June to September) to witness the enchanting spectacle of butterflies covering the trees and grounds.

Seven Springs (Epta Piges):

- Highlights: Seven Springs is a lush, verdant area where seven natural springs converge to create a small lake. The shaded path leading to the springs is ideal for a leisurely walk, and the cool, forested surroundings provide respite from the sun.
- Tunnel of Plane Trees: The highlight of Seven Springs is the "Tunnel of Plane Trees," a unique passage where the branches of plane trees create a shaded canopy over the footpath.

Mount Attavyros:

- Highlights: As the highest peak on Rhodes, Mount Attavyros offers a challenging hiking experience with rewarding panoramic views. The trail to the summit takes you through pine forests, and once at the top, you can enjoy breathtaking vistas of the island and the Aegean Sea.
- Flora and Fauna: The diverse vegetation on the mountain includes pine trees, cypress, and oak, providing a habitat for various bird species and unique plant life.

Monolithos Castle:

- Highlights: The hike to Monolithos Castle takes you through rugged landscapes with stunning views of the coastline. The castle itself, perched on a rocky outcrop, offers a glimpse into the island's medieval history.

- Seaside Exploration: After exploring the castle, descend to the nearby beach for a refreshing swim in the clear waters of the Aegean Sea.

Filerimos Hill (Ialyssos):

- Highlights: Filerimos Hill is home to the Church of Our Lady of Filerimos and an ancient acropolis. The cypress-lined path leading to the church provides a tranquil setting, and from the top, you can enjoy panoramic views of the surrounding landscapes.
- Golgothá: At the summit, discover Golgothá, a stone-carved representation of the crucifixion, adding a historical and cultural dimension to the hike.

Practical Tips for Hiking and Nature Exploration:

- Sturdy Footwear: Wear comfortable and sturdy hiking shoes suitable for different terrains, especially if you plan to explore trails with uneven surfaces.
- Water and Snacks: Carry sufficient water and snacks to stay hydrated and energized during your hikes, especially in areas where amenities may be limited.
- Sun Protection: Bring sunscreen, hats, and sunglasses to protect yourself from the sun, especially when hiking in exposed areas.
- Respect Nature: Follow designated paths, respect wildlife, and avoid disturbing the natural environment. Leave no trace and contribute to the preservation of Rhodes' natural beauty.

Exploring Rhodes on foot allows you to connect with its natural wonders, uncover hidden gems, and experience the island's diverse landscapes. Whether you choose the enchanting Valley of the Butterflies, the challenging ascent of Mount Attavyros, or the historical trails leading to Monolithos Castle, Rhodes' hiking trails promise a journey of discovery and connection with nature.

Water Activities and Excursions: Aquatic Adventures

Rhodes, surrounded by the crystal-clear waters of the Aegean Sea, offers a playground for water enthusiasts. From thrilling water sports to leisurely boat excursions, the island provides a diverse range of aquatic adventures, ensuring there's something for everyone seeking the embrace of the sea.

Windsurfing and Kitesurfing (Prasonisi):

- Highlights: Prasonisi, where the Aegean and Mediterranean seas meet, is a windsurfing and kitesurfing paradise. The strong winds create ideal conditions for these exhilarating water sports, making it a hotspot for enthusiasts of all skill levels.
- Windsurfing Schools: Beginners can take advantage of windsurfing schools in the area, offering lessons and equipment rental to get started in the thrilling world of wind and waves.

Snorkeling in Anthony Quinn Bay (Faliraki):

- Highlights: Anthony Quinn Bay, with its emerald-green waters and rocky formations, provides an excellent snorkeling experience. Explore the underwater world teeming with marine life, including colorful fish and vibrant sea plants.

- Snorkeling Gear: Bring your snorkeling gear or rent equipment from local shops to fully enjoy the underwater beauty of this picturesque bay.

Boat Tours and Island Hopping:

- Highlights: Embark on a boat tour to explore the coastline, hidden coves, and neighboring islands. From leisurely sailing trips to adventurous speedboat excursions, there are various options to choose from.
- Symi Island Day Trip: Take a day trip to Symi, a neighboring island known for its colorful architecture and charming harbor. Explore the narrow streets, visit the Monastery of the Archangel Michael, and savor local cuisine in the island's tavernas.

Scuba Diving (Kallithea Springs):

- Highlights: Kallithea Springs, with its underwater caves and clear waters, is a popular spot for scuba diving. Dive into the depths to discover marine life, ancient ruins, and the unique underwater landscapes of the Aegean.
- Diving Centers: Several diving centers around the island offer guided dives, courses for beginners, and equipment rental, making it accessible for both seasoned divers and those new to the underwater world.

Sea Kayaking in Lindos Bay:

- Highlights: Explore the coastline and hidden caves of Lindos Bay through sea kayaking. Paddle at your own pace, taking in the breathtaking views of the Acropolis of Lindos from the sea.

- Sunset Kayaking: Some operators offer sunset kayaking tours, providing a magical experience as the sun dips below the horizon, casting a warm glow over the waters.

Practical Tips for Water Activities:

- Safety First: Adhere to safety guidelines and instructions provided by instructors, especially for activities like windsurfing, scuba diving, and other water sports.
- Equipment Check: Before engaging in any water activity, ensure that your equipment is in good condition. This includes life jackets, snorkeling gear, and any other gear provided by operators.
- Booking in Advance: For popular excursions and guided activities, consider booking in advance to secure your spot, especially during peak tourist seasons.
- Weather Awareness: Be mindful of weather conditions, especially for boat tours and water activities. Some excursions may be weather-dependent, so it's essential to check forecasts before planning.

Rhodes' aquatic adventures provide a dynamic way to experience the island's coastal beauty and engage in thrilling water sports. Whether you're gliding over the waves in Prasonisi, snorkeling in the vibrant underwater world of Anthony Quinn Bay, or embarking on a boat excursion to Symi, each activity offers a unique perspective on the enchanting waters surrounding Rhodes.

Nightlife and Entertainment Hotspots in Rhodes

Exploring the nightlife in Rhodes offers a vibrant mix of traditional Greek hospitality, modern bars, and lively nightclubs. Here's a detailed guide to some of the top recommended nightlife and entertainment hotspots with their locations:

Rhodes Town:

1. Bar Street (Orfanidou Street):

Location: Rhodes Town, Old Town

- Description: Bar Street is the heart of nightlife in Rhodes Town. Lined with bars and clubs, it comes alive in the evening. Popular choices include Colorado Club and Camelot.

2. The Palace Bar:

Location: Ippokratous Square, Rhodes Town

- Description: Nestled in the historic square, The Palace Bar offers a laid-back atmosphere and great cocktails. Perfect for a relaxed evening.

3. Socratous Garden:

Location: Sokratous Street, Rhodes Town

- Description: A charming garden bar with a diverse drink menu. Ideal for those who prefer a more tranquil setting.

10.2 Lindos:

4. Amphitheatre Club:

Location: Lindos

- Description: Overlooking the Acropolis, Amphitheatre Club is a popular open-air club with a fantastic atmosphere and DJ performances.

5. Yiannis Bar:

Location: Lindos Main Square

- Description: A family-run bar with a warm atmosphere, Yiannis Bar is known for its friendly service and live music.

Faliraki:

6. Club Bed:

Location: Faliraki

- Description: One of the largest and most popular clubs in Faliraki, Club Bed hosts renowned DJs and offers a lively atmosphere.

7. Liquid Club:

Location: Faliraki

- Description: Known for its vibrant parties and themed nights, Liquid Club is a favorite among those seeking a high-energy nightlife experience.

Ialysos:

8. Buddha Lounge Bar:

Location: Ialysos

- Description: Offering a fusion of Asian and Mediterranean flavors, Buddha Lounge Bar is perfect for a more sophisticated evening.

Kallithea:

9. Kalithea Springs:

Location: Kallithea

- Description: While known for its historical significance, Kalithea Springs transforms into an elegant venue in the evenings, hosting events and parties.

Tips for Nightlife in Rhodes:

- Dress Code: Some venues may have a dress code, especially in upscale areas. It's advisable to check in advance.
- Theme Nights: Many clubs and bars have theme nights, so inquire about special events during your stay.
- Local Drinks: Don't miss trying local drinks and cocktails unique to Rhodes.
- Transportation: Ensure you have a plan for transportation back to your accommodation, especially if you're staying outside the main nightlife areas.

Rhodes offers a diverse and lively nightlife scene catering to various tastes. Whether you're into vibrant clubbing, relaxed garden bars, or beachside lounges, the island has something for everyone. Explore the different areas, soak in the atmosphere, and make the most of your nights in Rhodes!

Chapter 9

Unveiling Hidden Gems

Off-the-Beaten-Path Discoveries: Secrets of Rhodes

While Rhodes is celebrated for its well-known attractions, the island also hides treasures away from the popular tourist trails. Embark on a journey of discovery to unveil the hidden gems of Rhodes, where history, nature, and authentic local experiences converge.

Kritinia Castle:

- Location: Nestled on the western coast of Rhodes, Kritinia Castle offers panoramic views of the Aegean Sea and the neighboring islands.
- Highlights: This medieval castle, perched on a hill, provides a sense of solitude and a connection to Rhodes' rich history. Explore the ruins and savor the breathtaking sunset over the sea.

Agios Isidoros Monastery:

- Location: Tucked away in the interior of the island, Agios Isidoros Monastery is a serene retreat surrounded by olive groves.
- Highlights: The monastery, dedicated to Saint Isidoros, features a charming chapel and a peaceful courtyard. The tranquil ambiance and the scent of olive trees create a haven for contemplation.

Fourni Beach:

- Location: Fourni Beach is a secluded gem on the southern coast of Rhodes, accessible by boat or a scenic hike.
- Highlights: This hidden cove boasts crystal-clear waters and a pebble beach framed by rocky cliffs. It's an ideal spot for a quiet swim, away from the bustling crowds.

Ladiko Beach and Anthony Quinn's Bay:

- Location: Situated near Faliraki, Ladiko Beach and Anthony Quinn's Bay are lesser-known alternatives to more popular beaches.
- Highlights: Ladiko Beach, with its small bay and emerald waters, is a tranquil escape. Anthony Quinn's Bay, named after the actor, captivates with its unique underwater landscape, perfect for snorkeling.

Dimilia Village:

- Location: Tucked in the hills near Archangelos, Dimilia is a traditional village with cobblestone streets and well-preserved architecture.
- Highlights: Stroll through the narrow alleys, interact with friendly locals, and visit the traditional kafeneio (coffee shop) for an authentic taste of village life.

Kamiros Skala:

- Location: South of the village of Kritinia, Kamiros Skala is a tranquil harbor with a small fishing community.
- Highlights: Experience the charm of a traditional Greek fishing village, where colorful boats line the harbor, and waterfront tavernas serve freshly caught seafood.

Asklipio Castle:

- Location: Asklipio Castle stands on a hill in the southern part of Rhodes, offering commanding views of the surrounding landscapes.
- Highlights: This lesser-known castle provides a peaceful setting to explore historical remnants and enjoy a serene panorama that extends to the coast.

Tips for Exploring Hidden Gems:

- Local Recommendations: Consult locals or small guesthouses for recommendations on hidden gems. They often have insights into lesser-known places off the typical tourist routes.
- Exploration on Foot: Some hidden gems are best discovered by taking leisurely walks or hikes. Lace up your walking shoes and explore the lesser-explored paths.
- Timing: Visit these hidden gems during off-peak hours or seasons to experience them in a more serene and authentic atmosphere.
- Respect Nature and Locals: When exploring off-the-beaten-path locations, practice responsible tourism. Respect nature, local communities, and historical sites to ensure they remain unspoiled for future visitors.

Venture beyond the well-trodden paths, and you'll discover that Rhodes has a wealth of hidden gems waiting to be explored. Whether it's the solitude of Kritinia Castle, the authentic charm of Dimilia Village, or the tranquil beauty of Fourni Beach, these off-the-beaten-path discoveries add a layer of mystery and enchantment to your Rhodes experience.

Charming Villages and Local Encounters: Authentic Rhodes

Rhodes is not just about its historical landmarks; it's also a tapestry of charming villages that offer an authentic glimpse into local life. Explore these hidden gems, each with its unique character, warm hospitality, and a touch of traditional Greek charm.

Archangelos:

- Characteristics: Archangelos is a vibrant village known for its traditional architecture, lively squares, and the imposing Archangel Michael Castle.
- Local Encounters: Engage with locals at the village square, where you can find traditional kafeneia (coffee shops) and tavernas. Visit the castle for panoramic views and a deeper connection to the village's history.

Embonas:

- Characteristics: Nestled on the slopes of Mount Attavyros, Embonas is renowned for its wine production, offering a taste of the island's viticulture.
- Local Encounters: Visit local wineries to sample the region's wines, and don't miss the opportunity to join traditional festivals where music, dance, and local cuisine converge.

Kritinia:

- Characteristics: Kritinia is a picturesque village with narrow streets, traditional houses, and the medieval Kritinia Castle overlooking the Aegean Sea.

- Local Encounters: Explore the village's alleys, interact with friendly locals, and savor authentic Greek dishes in family-run tavernas. The castle offers not just history but also breathtaking sunset views.

Salakos:

- Characteristics: Salakos is a charming village surrounded by lush greenery and overlooked by the ancient Acropolis of Kamiros.
- Local Encounters: Wander through the village, known for its traditional houses adorned with colorful flowers. Taste local specialties, such as souma (a traditional spirit), and experience the warm hospitality of the locals.

Lachania:

- Characteristics: Lachania is a well-preserved village with stone-built houses, cobbled streets, and a tranquil atmosphere.
- Local Encounters: Stroll through the village square, where you'll find traditional cafes and tavernas. The authentic ambiance and welcoming locals provide a serene escape from the bustling tourist areas.

Siana:

- Characteristics: Siana is a mountain village surrounded by olive groves and vineyards, offering a serene retreat in the heart of Rhodes.
- Local Encounters: Visit the village during the festival of Virgin Mary (Panagia), where locals celebrate with traditional music, dancing, and feasting. Explore the local craft shops for unique souvenirs.

Tips for Authentic Village Exploration:

- Local Festivals: Check the local calendar for village festivals and events, where you can experience traditional music, dance, and culinary delights.
- Cultural Respect: When visiting villages, be mindful of local customs and traditions. Respect the privacy of residents and seek permission before taking photographs in certain situations.
- Language Connection: Engage with locals using basic Greek phrases. This effort is appreciated and can lead to more enriching interactions.
- Explore on Foot: Villages are often best explored on foot. Wander through the narrow streets, interact with locals, and embrace the unhurried pace of village life.

Rhodes' charming villages offer an authentic escape, allowing you to step into the daily rhythms of local life. Whether it's the lively squares of Archangelos, the wine culture of Embonas, or the tranquility of Lachania, each village has its own story to tell and welcomes visitors with open arms.

Rhodes' Best-Kept Secrets: Hidden Treasures Unveiled

Beyond the well-trodden paths and popular attractions, Rhodes harbors some of its best-kept secrets—hidden treasures waiting to be discovered. These lesser-known gems offer a unique perspective on the island's history, natural beauty, and cultural richness.

Old Hydrothermal Baths in Kallithea:

- Location: Tucked away in the bay of Kallithea, the Old Hydrothermal Baths are a hidden architectural marvel.
- Highlights: Built in the 1920s, these baths were once a luxurious retreat. Today, the intricate mosaic floors and elegant archways create a captivating atmosphere. The site often surprises visitors with its blend of history and serene coastal surroundings.

Prophet Elias Chapel in Faliraki:

- Location: Perched on a hill overlooking Faliraki, Prophet Elias Chapel is a charming hidden gem.
- Highlights: The chapel itself is a modest yet picturesque structure, but it's the panoramic views from the hill that make this spot special. Catch a sunrise or sunset to witness the landscape bathed in soft hues.

Marianthi Lighthouse in Kattavia:

- Location: The Marianthi Lighthouse stands proudly on the southern tip of Rhodes in Kattavia.
- Highlights: A less-explored destination, this lighthouse offers breathtaking views of the rugged coastline and the endless blue of the Aegean Sea. The sense of isolation adds to the charm, making it a perfect spot for solitude and reflection.

Monastery of Panagia Ipseni in Laerma:

- Location: Nestled in the village of Laerma, the Monastery of Panagia Ipseni is a hidden spiritual retreat.
- Highlights: This small monastery, dedicated to the Virgin Mary, exudes tranquility. The scenic surroundings and the

simplicity of the monastery make it a peaceful sanctuary away from the crowds.

Ancient Stadium in Ialysos:

- Location: Unearthed near the village of Trianda, the Ancient Stadium of Ialysos is an archaeological gem.
- Highlights: Dating back to the Hellenistic period, this stadium once hosted athletic competitions. The site is still in the process of excavation, allowing visitors a glimpse into the island's ancient sporting history.

Mount Profitis Ilias Cave:

- Location: Concealed within the folds of Mount Profitis Ilias, the cave is a well-hidden natural wonder.
- Highlights: The cave, adorned with stalactites and stalagmites, creates a mystical atmosphere. The trek to reach it adds an element of adventure, rewarding intrepid explorers with a subterranean spectacle.

Tips for Discovering Rhodes' Best-Kept Secrets:

- Local Guidance: Seek recommendations from locals, especially in smaller villages or less touristy areas. They may share insights into hidden spots that aren't widely known.
- Off-Peak Exploration: Visit these secrets during off-peak hours or seasons to enjoy them without crowds, enhancing the sense of discovery.
- Respect and Preservation: When visiting lesser-known sites, practice responsible tourism. Respect the natural and cultural heritage to ensure these hidden treasures remain preserved for future generations.

- Flexible Itinerary: Allow for flexibility in your itinerary to explore unexpected discoveries. Sometimes, the best experiences come from spontaneous detours.

Rhodes' best-kept secrets add an element of mystery and wonder to your journey. Whether you're uncovering the Old Hydrothermal Baths in Kallithea, witnessing the beauty from Prophet Elias Chapel, or exploring the ancient stadium in Ialysos, these hidden treasures enrich your Rhodes adventure with a sense of exploration and awe.

Chapter 10

Practical Information and Resources

Essential Contacts and Emergency Information

When exploring Rhodes, it's crucial to have access to essential contacts and emergency information to ensure a safe and seamless travel experience. Familiarize yourself with the following contacts and resources for your time on the island:

Emergency Services:

- Medical Emergencies: In case of a medical emergency, dial 166 for immediate assistance. The operators can provide guidance and dispatch medical help to your location.
- Police Assistance: For police assistance or reporting incidents, dial 100. The local police can address a range of issues, from lost belongings to more serious concerns.
- Fire Department: Dial 199 if you encounter a fire or any related emergency. The fire department is equipped to handle fire incidents and related safety concerns.

Tourist Police:

- Tourist Police Hotline: If you are a tourist in need of assistance, you can contact the Tourist Police by dialing 171. They are specifically trained to assist visitors and provide support in various situations.

Medical Facilities:

- General Hospitals: Rhodes has several general hospitals equipped to handle a range of medical issues. The main hospital is the General Hospital of Rhodes, located in Rhodes Town. Another notable hospital is the Archangelos General Hospital.

- Pharmacies: Throughout the island, you'll find pharmacies (Farmakeia) where you can purchase over-the-counter medications and consult with pharmacists. In case of non-urgent medical issues, pharmacies are valuable resources.

Embassies and Consulates:

- Contact Information: Take note of the contact information for your embassy or consulate in Greece. They can assist with various matters, including lost passports, legal issues, and emergencies.

Local Transport:

- Public Transportation: For information on buses and schedules, contact the local bus company. Taxis are also readily available; note down reliable taxi services or apps for convenient transportation.
- Car Rentals: If you've rented a car, keep the contact information for the car rental agency, including emergency assistance numbers and details on what to do in case of breakdowns or accidents.

Local Tourism Offices:

- Rhodes Tourism Office: Visit the official tourism office in Rhodes Town for maps, brochures, and information on local attractions. The staff can provide valuable insights and assistance.

Communication Services:

- Mobile Networks: Rhodes has reliable mobile network coverage. If you're using a local SIM card, keep the customer service number of your mobile provider for assistance.
- Internet Access: Most accommodations, cafes, and public spaces offer Wi-Fi. If you encounter connectivity issues, check with your accommodation or local establishments for support.

Weather Information:

- Weather Updates: Stay informed about the weather forecast, especially if you plan outdoor activities. Weather updates are available through local news channels, online platforms, or weather apps.

Currency and Banking:

- Local Currency: The official currency in Greece is the Euro (€). Keep the contact information for your bank in case of card issues or if you need to inform them about your travel dates.

Language Assistance:

- Translation Services: In case of language barriers, note down contact information for translation services or language assistance. This can be useful for effective communication.

Tips for Emergency Preparedness:

- Document Copies: Carry photocopies of essential documents, including your passport, travel insurance, and emergency contacts. Store digital copies securely as well.

- Local Area Knowledge: Familiarize yourself with the layout of the local area, including the location of your accommodation, nearby medical facilities, and emergency exits.
- Language Basics: Learn a few basic Greek phrases related to emergencies, such as "help," "emergency," and "I need assistance."
- Local Customs: Understand local customs regarding emergency services. In some countries, it might be customary to contact the local police first in certain situations.

Being prepared and having quick access to essential contacts ensures that you can navigate any challenges that may arise during your stay in Rhodes. Whether it's a medical concern, lost belongings, or language barriers, having the right information at your fingertips enhances your ability to handle situations effectively and with confidence.

Recommended Reading and Resources

Before embarking on your journey to Rhodes, diving into some recommended reading materials and resources can enhance your understanding of the island's history, culture, and attractions. Here's a curated list of books, online resources, and travel guides to enrich your pre-trip preparations:

Books:

"The Colossus of Maroussi" by Henry Miller:

- Description: Henry Miller's travel narrative captures his experiences in Greece, providing poetic insights into the country's culture and landscapes.

"Rhodes: The Island of the Knights" by Mark Ellingham:

- Description: A comprehensive guidebook that delves into Rhodes' history, architecture, and cultural heritage, offering practical information for travelers.

"The Dodecanese: A Traveller's Guide to the Islands of the Aegean" by Lawrence Durrell:

- Description: Lawrence Durrell explores the islands of the Dodecanese, including Rhodes, in this travelogue, providing a literary journey through the region.

Online Resources:

Rhodes Tourism Official Website:

Website: Rhodes Tourism Official Website

- Description: The official tourism website offers up-to-date information on attractions, events, and practical details for visitors.

Lonely Planet Rhodes:

Website: Lonely Planet Rhodes

- Description: Lonely Planet provides valuable insights, travel tips, and destination guides for Rhodes.

TripAdvisor Rhodes Forum:

Website: TripAdvisor Rhodes Forum

- Description: The Rhodes forum on TripAdvisor allows travelers to share experiences, ask questions, and seek advice from others who have visited the island.

Travel Guides:

Rick Steves Greece: Athens & the Peloponnese:

- Description: Rick Steves' travel guide offers practical advice and cultural insights for exploring Greece, including Rhodes.

DK Eyewitness Travel Guide: Greek Islands:

- Description: The DK Eyewitness guide provides detailed information on the Greek Islands, with sections dedicated to Rhodes and its attractions.

National Geographic Traveler: Greece:

- Description: National Geographic's travel guide to Greece offers stunning visuals and in-depth information on the country's regions, including Rhodes.

Educational Websites:

Greek National Tourism Organization:

Website: Visit Greece

- Description: The Greek National Tourism Organization's official website provides general information about Greece, travel tips, and insights into various regions.

Encyclopaedia Britannica - Rhodes:

Website: Rhodes - Encyclopaedia Britannica

- Description: Britannica's online resource offers historical and geographical information about Rhodes.

Blogs and Travel Journals:

Rhodes Travel Blog by Matt Barrett:

Blog: Rhodes Travel Blog

- Description: A blog with personal insights and travel tips for Rhodes, authored by experienced traveler Matt Barrett.

The Trusted Traveller - Rhodes Travel Guide:

Blog: Rhodes Travel Guide

- Description: The Trusted Traveller offers a detailed guide to Rhodes, including practical advice and recommendations.

Tips for Using Resources:

- Diverse Perspectives: Explore a variety of resources to gain diverse perspectives on Rhodes. Books, travel guides, and online forums provide different insights and information.
- Latest Updates: Check for the latest editions of guidebooks and online resources to ensure that you have the most up-to-date information.
- Community Recommendations: Pay attention to recommendations and insights shared by fellow travelers on forums and blogs. Personal experiences can offer valuable insights.
- Cultural Context: Seek resources that delve into the cultural context of Rhodes, helping you appreciate the island's history, traditions, and local way of life.

By immersing yourself in recommended reading materials and online resources, you'll be well-equipped with knowledge about Rhodes, making your journey more informed and enriching. Whether you prefer historical narratives, practical guides, or firsthand travel experiences, these resources offer a wealth of information to enhance your exploration of the island.

Sustainable Travel Tips for Rhodes

As a responsible traveler exploring the beautiful island of Rhodes, it's essential to adopt sustainable practices that contribute to the preservation of the environment, culture, and local communities. Embrace these sustainable travel tips to make a positive impact during your journey:

Respect Nature and Wildlife:

- Stay on Designated Paths: When hiking or exploring natural areas, stick to designated paths to minimize your impact on the environment.
- Avoid Disturbing Wildlife: Observe wildlife from a distance and avoid disrupting their natural behaviors. Resist the temptation to feed or approach animals closely.

Conserve Water and Energy:

- Limit Water Usage: Conserve water by taking shorter showers and using water sparingly. Report any leaks or water wastage to your accommodation.
- Turn Off Lights and Electronics: Be mindful of energy consumption by turning off lights, air conditioning, and electronics when not in use. Consider unplugging chargers when they're not actively charging devices.

Reduce, Reuse, Recycle:

- Use Reusable Items: Bring a reusable water bottle, shopping bag, and utensils to minimize single-use plastic waste.

- Recycle Properly: Familiarize yourself with local recycling practices and use designated bins for recyclables. If recycling options are limited, consider carrying your recyclables until you find an appropriate disposal point.

Support Local Businesses:

- Choose Local Products: Opt for locally-made souvenirs and products to support the island's economy. Visit local markets and shops to contribute directly to the community.
- Dine at Local Eateries: Explore traditional tavernas and restaurants that showcase local cuisine. This not only supports local businesses but also allows you to savor authentic flavors.

Cultural Respect:

- Respect Historical Sites: When visiting historical sites and monuments, follow the rules and guidelines to preserve these cultural treasures. Avoid touching or leaning on fragile structures.
- Dress Appropriately: Respect local customs and dress modestly when visiting religious sites or conservative communities. This demonstrates cultural sensitivity.

Use Sustainable Transportation:

- Public Transport and Walking: Utilize public transportation, walk, or bike to explore the island. This helps reduce carbon emissions and allows you to experience the destination at a leisurely pace.
- Choose Eco-friendly Tours: Opt for eco-friendly and sustainable tour operators that prioritize responsible practices and minimize environmental impact.

Educate Yourself:

- Learn About Local Conservation Efforts: Take the time to learn about local conservation initiatives and efforts to protect the environment. Support organizations or activities that contribute positively to sustainability.
- Understand Cultural Norms: Familiarize yourself with local customs and norms to ensure your actions align with cultural expectations. This includes appropriate behavior in public spaces and interactions with locals.

Minimize Plastic Usage:

- Say No to Single-Use Plastics: Refuse single-use plastics such as straws, plastic bags, and disposable cutlery. Carry a reusable shopping bag and say no to unnecessary plastic items.
- Participate in Beach Cleanups: If possible, join or organize beach cleanups to contribute to the preservation of marine environments.

Offset Your Carbon Footprint:

- Support Carbon Offset Programs: Consider supporting carbon offset programs to compensate for the environmental impact of your travels. Many organizations offer options to invest in sustainable projects that reduce carbon emissions.

Engage in Responsible Wildlife Tourism:

- Research Animal Encounters: If considering wildlife encounters, choose activities that prioritize animal welfare and conservation. Avoid experiences that involve exploitation or harm to animals.

Leave No Trace:

- Pack Out Your Waste: Ensure you leave no trace of your presence by packing out all waste, including food scraps and litter. Dispose of waste in designated bins.

By integrating these sustainable travel tips into your journey, you contribute to the well-being of Rhodes and leave a positive footprint on the environment and local communities. Sustainable travel practices not only enhance your travel experience but also play a crucial role in preserving the charm and authenticity of this beautiful island for future generations.

Chapter 11

Conclusion

Reflecting on Your Rhodes Experience

As your journey on the captivating island of Rhodes comes to a close, take a moment to reflect on the unique experiences, cultural discoveries, and natural wonders you've encountered. Reflecting on your Rhodes experience allows you to appreciate the richness of the island and the memories you've created. Consider the following aspects as you wrap up your adventure:

Cultural Immersion:

Diverse Heritage: Reflect on the diverse heritage of Rhodes, from its ancient roots to the medieval grandeur and the influences of different civilizations. Consider the cultural tapestry you've explored.

Natural Beauty:

Geographical Marvels: Think about the geographical marvels you've witnessed, from the coastal wonders to the inland beauty of mountains and valleys. Recall the serene landscapes and breathtaking views.

Local Connections:

Charming Villages: Remember the moments spent in charming villages, interacting with locals, experiencing their traditions, and savoring the authenticity of village life.

Gastronomic Journey:

Culinary Delights: Reflect on the gastronomic journey you've embarked on, indulging in the savory delights of Rhodes cuisine. Consider the unique flavors and local specialties you've tasted.

Hidden Gems:

Off-the-Beaten-Path Discoveries: Revisit the off-the-beaten-path discoveries and hidden gems you've explored. Contemplate the sense of adventure and wonder that comes with discovering lesser-known treasures.

Sustainable Travel:

Positive Impact: Consider the sustainable travel practices you've adopted and the positive impact you've made on the environment, local communities, and cultural preservation.

Memorable Moments:

Personal Highlights: Recall the personal highlights and memorable moments that have made your Rhodes experience truly special. Whether it's a sunset over the sea, a cultural festival, or a quiet village stroll, cherish these memories.

Growth and Learning:

Travel Insights: Reflect on the insights gained and lessons learned during your journey. Travel has a unique way of broadening perspectives and fostering personal growth.

Farewell and Best Wishes for Future Adventures

As you bid farewell to Rhodes, let it be a not a goodbye, but a "see you later." The memories and experiences you've gathered will stay with you, enriching your life with the essence of this remarkable island. Here are some heartfelt wishes for your future adventures:

May Your Journeys Be Ever Inspiring:

May your future travels be as inspiring and fulfilling as your time in Rhodes. May each destination unfold new wonders and broaden your horizons.

Embrace the Spirit of Exploration:

Continue to embrace the spirit of exploration and curiosity. There is a world full of diverse cultures, landscapes, and experiences waiting for you.

Savor Every Moment:

May you savor every moment of your future adventures, cherishing the beauty of different places, the warmth of new connections, and the joy of discovery.

Carry the Wisdom of Travel:

Carry the wisdom of travel with you— the ability to adapt, the openness to different perspectives, and the appreciation for the beauty found in every corner of the world.

Create Lifelong Memories:

May your future journeys be filled with joy, laughter, and the creation of lifelong memories. Travel has a unique way of shaping our lives, and may each adventure be a chapter in your personal story.

Safe and Fulfilling Travels:

Wishing you safe and fulfilling travels wherever your path may lead. May you continue to explore, learn, and find joy in the journey.

As you venture forth from Rhodes, remember that the world is vast and full of wonders. Carry the spirit of Rhodes with you—its history, its beauty, and the warmth of its people—knowing that the memories you've collected will forever be a part of your travel tapestry. Farewell, and may your future adventures be as extraordinary as the one you've had on this enchanting island.

Printed in Great Britain
by Amazon

36646657R00076